PRAISE FOR *STREAMS OF CONSEQUENCE*:

"This is a beautifully written, wise book. Lorne Fitch uses his expert knowledge of Alberta wildlife species and spaces to inspire us with their ecological importance and beauty. And he draws on his inside experience to smarten us all up regarding dynamic inaction versus meaningful steps to conserve them. Lorne's book deserves a broad readership – for the lessons it holds not just for Alberta, but for our country and planet."

— MONTE HUMMEL, President Emeritus,
World Wildlife Fund–Canada

"Lorne Fitch writes with the deep insights of a lifelong biologist, the wisdom of an elder and the wry humour of a Stephen Leacock. This is a work that belongs on every bookshelf, between the works of Aldo Leopold and Gregory Clark: a rich compilation of thoughtful, enlightening and frequently humorous reflections on the wild nature of western Canada, and the urgent need to care for it better. This book, by one of Canada's most legendary conservationists and outdoorsmen, was well worth waiting for. It's destined to become a Canadian classic."

— KEVIN VAN TIGHEM, former Superintendent of Banff National Park, ecologist, and author of *Bears Without Fear, Heart Waters: Sources of the Bow River, Our Place: Changing the Nature of Alberta* and *Wild Roses Are Worth It: Reimagining the Alberta Advantage*

"From the width of the horned lizard's home range, to the hectares of lost trout spawning habitat, to the depth of soil erosion caused by off-road vehicles, Lorne Fitch has taken deeply personal measurements of Alberta's ecology, and our relationship to it. This is the work of a truly omnivorous mind, sprinkled with engaging quotes that range from Aldo Leopold to Marcel Proust to the author's mother."

— DON GAYTON, ecologist and author of
The Wheatgrass Mechanism and *The Sky and the Patio*

"With these engaging essays Lorne Fitch testifies to the costs the natural world has paid for the prosperity realized from exploiting natural resources. Whether Fitch writes about the native prairie or the Eastern Slopes of the Rocky Mountains he details the natural gems we have lost, tarnished or threatened. His language is stinging and evocative, his analysis infuriating and inspiring. Fitch's essays, by nurturing our sense of wonder and responsibility for the natural world, invite citizens and governments alike to see the world differently. He invites us to embrace the attitudinal and policy changes needed to bestow greater privilege to the needs of the natural world in our future."

— DR. IAN URQUHART, Professor Emeritus, University of Alberta

STREAMS OF CONSEQUENCE

Streams
of
Consequence

DISPATCHES FROM THE CONSERVATION WORLD

LORNE FITCH, P. Biol.

RMB

For information on purchasing bulk quantities of this book, or to obtain media
excerpts or invite the author to speak at an event, please visit rmbooks.com and
select the "Contact" tab.

RMB | Rocky Mountain Books Ltd.
rmbooks.com
@rmbooks
facebook.com/rmbooks

Cataloguing data available from Library and Archives Canada
ISBN 9781771606691 (softcover)
ISBN 9781771606707 (electronic)

Design: Lara Minja, Lime Design
Cover photo: Jean Beaufort/Wikimedia Commons

Printed and bound in Canada

We acknowledge the financial support of the Government of Canada through
the Canada Book Fund and the Canada Council for the Arts, and of the province
of British Columbia through the British Columbia Arts Council and the Book
Publishing Tax Credit.

DISCLAIMER
The views expressed in this book are those of the author and do not necessarily
reflect those of the publishing company, its staff, or its affiliates.

We would like to also take this opportunity to acknowledge the traditional territories upon which we live and work. In Calgary, Alberta, we acknowledge the Niitsítapi (Blackfoot) and the people of the Treaty 7 region in Southern Alberta, which includes the Siksika, the Piikuni, the Kainai, the Tsuut'ina, and the Stoney Nakoda First Nations, including Chiniki, Bearpaw, and Wesley First Nations. The City of Calgary is also home to Métis Nation of Alberta, Region III. In Victoria, British Columbia, we acknowledge the traditional territories of the Lkwungen (Esquimalt and Songhees), Malahat, Pacheedaht, Scia'new, T'Sou-ke, and W̱SÁNEĆ (Pauquachin, Tsartlip, Tsawout, Tseycum) peoples.

Contents

Introduction

You can't go back and change the beginning,
but you can start where you are at,
and change the ending.

— C.S. Lewis

There is a sense, maybe convention, that as a scientist one must be dispassionate, objective, above the fray and coldly clinical, dispensing "just the facts, ma'am." Science can inform us what has happened, what is happening and what is likely to happen, given trends and trajectories.

What science can't do, it seems, is make us do anything about the information. I believe one essential task of science, and of biologists, is to advocate, to lobby, to passionately engage in essential debates with ecological knowledge.

When we're viewing through an economic lens, everything seems possible. When viewed through an ecological one, many economic dreams become nightmares. Whatever our decisions and choices are, there will be streams of consequence. Timely information might incite people to understand limits and press for policy, legislation and enforcement to protect ecological integrity.

The following essays and stories form both metaphor and morality. They deal with how we perceive things and the question, How do we behave based on our perceptions? Some bits (and bites) of ecological knowledge are a starting point for perceptual shifts in our thinking and ultimately our actions. The purpose behind writing about issues isn't just to inform people, but to get them mad enough to do something.

Writing also has a role in making people look, one more time, at something they have looked at dozens of times, to enable them to see something different. Sometimes we don't notice what we see every day.

There are places where stories have always been more than mere fiction, more than entertainment and more than a way to pass the time. They have been the mechanism for people to understand their past, shape their present and give context for the future. For some, the landscape is carved with legends. There is a myth behind every mountain, a tale to match every stream, and even the trees form part of the narrative. We need that amalgam of imagination, memory, literature and history. In places where there has not been time to develop these stories, we lose our connection to the landscape and, indeed, to the critical pieces of it.

Biology derives its power not from technology, or the wizardry of mathematical models, certainly not through the arcane language of science, but through the connections and relationships we build with the natural world and its occupants. Curiosity is a portal to raising concern; blind acceptance and acquiescence block people from asking the necessary questions.

The landscape is a broad canvas upon which, over time, we paint our wants and desires. We are very much artists of the moment, seeing only the slice of canvas in front of us, and not so much the portion before, or after. There was a time when the air didn't smell of greed and gasoline, when the water wasn't gritty between your teeth, the soil wasn't paved over, and the forests weren't stumps, sawdust and sediment. Landscapes suffer because we value our immediate prejudices more than clean water, quiet, and abundant fish and wildlife.

How do we know who we are if we don't look in the mirror called the landscape? The mirror is the land, the water and the wildlife. An objective look tells us how we have treated this place called Alberta. The outcome of the examination reveals who we are.

Writing about the abused landscapes of the province is like walking through an untended graveyard. There are no quick fixes, no silver bullets, no cosmetic floral arrangements and no magic legislation. The solutions, like those for an addict, have to come from within, from making better personal, political and corporate choices.

I have a grounding in Alberta. Both my sets of grandparents were homesteaders, settling west of Red Deer at the dawning of the 20th century. I grew up on a farm near those family origins, when the countryside was still semi-wild. My somewhat feral childhood focused on wildlife and wild country. It was a logical progression to a career as a biologist. It means I have deep roots in Alberta, am concerned about the future of Alberta and am an advocate for an Alberta that retains some of what moulded me as a child. That passion is a motivation to write; experience provides credibility.

For years I have criss-crossed the province, learned the landscape, investigated fish and wildlife populations, and engaged with ranchers, landowners, industry and bureaucrats over conservation issues and opportunities. This included the inventory and research of trout streams from the Montana border to the North Saskatchewan watershed, work on fisheries and wildlife mitigation programs, supervising a demonstration ranch in the dry, mixed-grass prairie, riparian restoration work in all corners of the province, challenging logging and petroleum interests with better practices, being part of planning species at risk recovery, and engaging in environmental prosecutions. It was a unique position to be in, and this allows me to write about those experiences from an "insider's" viewpoint.

My wide-ranging experience and insights on conservation in Alberta now go back five decades. I have been in the "trade" long enough to be able to look back on the changes, weigh their significance, and write about where we came from, where we are at, and where the trend will take us, if we choose one road or another. I hope there is an appetite amongst Albertans (and others) for understanding the ecological crossroads we are at, and what needs to be done to retain our wild heritage.

While saving the environment ultimately, inevitably, is everyone's responsibility, it is the conservation community and scientists who need to provide the essential nudges. Governments react to public pressure, corporations won't move until legislation and the marketplace dictate change, and communities and individuals need information, support and motivation to make change happen.

For many years I have used my communication skills to give a voice to biologists and others engaged in conservation work who may not have the freedom of unfettered dialogue. To those people I dedicate this book.

Prologue

WHEN THE STRAWBERRY JAM BOOM WENT BUST

I'm going through a bit of a recession, maybe even verging on a depression. It has to do with strawberry jam, not with the markets. My mother-in-law, who has made arguably the best strawberry jam wherever in the world there are strawberries, has stopped cooking up this fruity elixir. This represents a serious downturn for me, a jam crunch.

She has her reasons: age and energy. I bear her no malice for the cessation of picking, cleaning, slicing, cooking and canning. There are better things to do on the hottest day of the year. But this was the underpinning, the substance that signalled the soundness of my breakfast world. The glue that held breakfast together is missing.

It has come to an end. My world, if not collapsed, is echoing with the sound of a spoon in an empty jar. No more coming back from southern Ontario with jars of it. No more well-wrapped jars arriving at Christmas. No more jammy care packages delivered by eastern family members to the poor, deprived westerners.

Our cupboards used to run over, our larder groaning under the accumulated weight. Jars of it piled up, engulfing us faster than we could engulf their contents. Jars of it matured on our shelves, developing their unique bouquets, coalescing into a whole that was greater than the parts.

We would ponder whether to open a bottle of the '97, a robust, fruity number, or throw caution to the wind and open the latest offerings. Jam would be shared with all of our friends. Sometimes we would push it, like some illicit substance that was rumoured to take you to another dimension. To our friends, most of whom grew up in the 1960s, this was too much to resist. Indeed, the bountiful surplus of strawberry jam was too much for me to resist.

How did I treat this cornucopia of jam? Sadly, my response was tinged with sarcasm, derision and thoughtlessness. "We've been bequeathed a lifetime supply of jam," I often opined to my wife, comparing the accumulated jars to some family legacy or inheritance. "More jam!" I would exclaim, with less than enthusiasm at the opening of a parcel containing – wait for it – more jam. "A clearance sale on jam," I would joke. "We're jammed up in our warehouse."

Callous, empty, stupid words! Profligate use has emptied the cupboard, and the shelves are bare. The strawberry jam train has long left the station. Not even the residual stickiness remains. All that sticks is the distant memory of that last precious jar.

A mood of despair, of longing and of trepidation for the future has set in. Because foresight isn't an option anymore, I've been beating myself up with hindsight. Why didn't I extol the virtues of her jam to my mother-in-law? Why didn't I appear more appreciative of her loving labours? And why didn't I encourage her in the continued manufacture of that ambrosia? Because, I guess, when in surplus one never thinks of shortage. The Chinese axiom that "every banquet comes to an end" never resonated when ladling that sweet concoction of berries onto toast.

"Sooner or later, everyone sits down to a banquet of consequences," said Robert Louis Stevenson, the 19th-century author of *Treasure Island.* He would not have known of my mother-in-law's strawberry jam. If he had, he surely would have identified it as a substance worthy of the title of treasure. But I did not, regrettably. My banquet is set, and it is void of strawberry jam.

If only I'd saved some, meted it out with a sense of conservation, been more judicious in sharing it, or thought about how to make the supply last longer. But I didn't. In my blindness, I thought the largesse would be endless. I thought the strawberry jam frontier would never end. The strawberry jam resource was, in my mind, unplumbed in its depth. The signals were there, of course, but I ignored them. Any distant early warning suggestions of showing restraint, of considering future jam eaters or of gaining self-sufficiency in the jam department were met with disdainful dismissal.

If I could have just one more chance, get one more jar, I promise I'll cherish it. I will never again consume strawberry jam like a pig at a trough. I will think about tomorrow and about the limited supply of that truly rare, valuable commodity.

I'll take care not to overuse this precious natural resource with careless disdain for the consequences. I'll steward this bequest with love and respect.

You may be on a different jam trajectory, one where you have time to evaluate and reassess your consumption. It's too late now for me to make amends, to turn back the hands of time, and watch the jam jars magically refill. I know now that I took things for granted when the jam economy was booming.

For the love of jam, please consider a change. Sit down with your jam maker; learn the craft. Grasp the jam torch and make sure it stays lit. Never forget how precious those jars of canned sunshine, rain and love are. I know I'll never take my mother-in-law's strawberry jam for granted again.

1
Things, Explained

Over the long haul of life on this planet it is the ecologists, and not the bookkeepers of business, who are the ultimate accountants.

— Steward Udall

UNINTENDED CONSEQUENCES

In the days when wildlife fell into categories of "good" and "bad," my cousin and I decided to chop down a tree with a magpie nest in it. We weren't bothered by thoughts of biodiversity or of the great web of life with all of the strands, connections and synergies of the multi-faceted parts of the world.

What motivated us was the thought of the cash bounty on each pair of magpie legs, offered by that eminent conservation organization, the Alberta Fish and Game Association. Never let it be thought that wildlife lacks value, especially to a pair of cash-poor and bloodthirsty farm kids. The nest was in the top of a tall aspen tree. We reasoned that, instead of us going up, the tree should come down. The externalizing of the cost of our endeavour to the environment never occurred to us.

With an axe dulled by decades of firewood splitting, we worried away at the tree until sometime after noon. We had managed to beaver our way through most of the trunk, but the tree, stubbornly, wouldn't fall down.

A coincident and synergistic series of events then began to unfold. The first was the arrival of my aunt to see why we had missed lunch, an inexplicable event in her view. The second was the development of a stiff breeze.

As my aunt started climbing over a barbed wire fence some dozens of yards from our worksite, the tree shifted with the wind. Giving us no time for the satisfaction of yelling "Timber!" it let go with an ear-splitting crack. With a whoosh of displaced air, it fell, straight down across the top of the fence. The great weight instantly tightened the loose top wire. Like a struck piano key, the reverberation sent a bow wave down the wire to where my aunt was in mid-passage over the fence. As the wire tightened, it lifted, propelling my aunt, a rather large woman, in an awe-inspiring airborne arc.

My cousin and I stood transfixed. Too many things were happening too quickly for us to grasp the significance of any of them, but we became quickly conversant with the principles of gravity and of ballistics, at least in terms of the trajectory of a heavy body.

Later, unable to sit because of our stinging backsides (this was in an era when spanking was not only socially acceptable but often viewed as mandatory), we were able to reflect on the lessons we had learned. These included, as I can still recall, that planning the fall line of a tree before the first axe blow is important. It also became apparent to us that picking a site a long way from adult view is a way to reduce the potential for retribution.

My aunt was, for some time, nervous around fences when the wind blew. She remained mute on whether she had gleaned something significant from the experience.

Someone with a large amount of scar tissue, perhaps from a similar life event, once reflected, "Nature is a hard teacher because she gives the test first, followed by the lesson." A fundamental lesson of unintended consequences is that, simply put, every choice comes with a consequence.

The forest reserves of Alberta are patterned with a lattice-work of roads, trails and utility corridors connecting logging clear-cuts, wellsites and random and formal recreation sites. In total, these pathways exceed the disturbances that native trout, carnivores and ungulates can bear. And because everything flows downhill, they affect the quality of water we drink.

This network of cuts began with a seemingly well-intentioned plan in the 1950s to build the Forestry Trunk Road, a thousand-kilometre gravel trail trending north-south through the foothills of the Rocky Mountains. Ostensibly, the rationale was that the road would aid in fighting forest fires, thus reducing their occurrence and size.

In classic unintended-consequence fashion, protecting the forest from all fires led to a dangerous buildup of fuel. With better access, more people roaming the land resulted in more wildfire starts. Instead of reducing the risk of fire, fires have become more prevalent and, often more severe, with greater consequences, not the desired result envisioned by early road planners.

The route of the Trunk Road (also called Highway 40) spurred on industrial incursions into the forest reserves and opened up previously inaccessible areas to motorized recreation. The catskinners who bulldozed the trail through an unroaded wilderness would scarcely recognize it today. The forest reserves, originally set up for watershed protection, have never been the same since.

I recall family trips in the late 1950s and early 1960s, when the road was still a narrow trail with grass growing up between the wheel tracks. Travelling the Trunk Road now is an excursion through a veil of thick dust, with the constant possibility of a logging truck or a massive motorhome emerging from the gloom.

When I've interviewed elderly anglers, they've spoken of exceptional fishing before and just after the road was completed. "There were so many trout you had to hide behind a tree to bait your hook," one recalled. Trout populations have since gone from abundant to imperilled. While fishing pressure probably contributed, one characteristic of unintended consequences is a cascade of events.

Erosion from a human land-use footprint, like logging clear-cuts and access trails, has long been recognized as a serious issue for fish. In a landmark paper published in 1961, biologists A.J. Cordone and D.W. Kelly documented the sediment waves associated with post–Second World War logging in California and concluded:

> More than anything else we need to develop a philosophy of land husbandry that will avoid the creation of untreated and running sores on the earth's surface. Man must acquire a responsibility to future generations that matches the power he has gained through the development of heavy machinery.
>
> ... Unless this can be done many of our trout streams will be destroyed by the deposition of sediment.

Erosion from land uses creates sediment yields greater than natural levels. Research results, which now span more than six decades, are exhaustive and categorical, yet they are unconscionably ignored as the logging footprint continues to bleed sediment. Newer insights also show that the land-use footprint speeds up runoff from snowmelt and rainfall, leading to greater flood risk for downstream communities. Given that backdrop, the consequences of many land-use decisions can hardly now be considered "unintended."

Unintended consequences, by definition, would be impossible to foresee and prevent. In reality, few are (like the felling of the aspen tree with the magpie nest), but we take scant notice of past events to accurately predict the effects of proposed actions. We are blinded by our development footprint (and the presumed rewards) because we can only imagine more must be better. As Aldo Leopold observed, it's a matter of "being too busy with new tinkerings to think of end effects."

Writer J.K. Rowling summarizes the thinking of most people with, "The consequences of our actions are always so complicated, so diverse, that predicting the future is a very difficult business indeed." Anticipating the consequences of our actions (and sometimes inactions) may seem overly complicated, unpredictable and unknowable, but it is not always impossible. There are ways to look ahead. We can use some rudimentary tools, like a map, or a mirror. Sometimes, by looking back, we can see ahead more clearly.

One mirror is history. We can reflect on past actions and their effects to foresee the possible outcome of a current decision. A key map is cumulative effects analysis, especially since it is often the piling on of the additive effects of several actions that have the greatest set of consequences.

There are tools to help us avoid the unintended consequences of imprudent, overenthusiastic or short-sighted endeavours. Without their use, we risk being lost in a sea of boosterism, economic determinism and unrealistic wishes. The outcomes of these can include degraded landscape integrity, fish and wildlife losses, unresolved land-use conflicts and reclamation costs borne by the Alberta taxpayer.

At all levels, the choices we make create an aftermath of consequences. Sometime after my aunt had recovered from her unscheduled flight, my cousin and I were sent out to repair the damaged fence, another unintended consequence of our actions. This was no small task, since it was now draped with a mature aspen tree. There hadn't been time when the tree fell to inspect the magpie nest, given all the commotion, trauma and retribution. After all of that, and in spite of the effort, the nest was empty!

THE INEQUITY OF "BALANCE"

I experienced the inequity of "balance" early in life. My mother would give my older brother a chocolate bar, to be shared "equally" with me. He would break the bar roughly in half, then nibble off the extraneous edges so the halves were even. If too much was removed from one piece, the other one required attention, to achieve "balance." Eventually we would each get the same amount, although he had a head start on the share.

In discussions about development and the environment, those on the side of development always argue for a "balanced" approach, meaning the environment has to give so they can get their share. I have flashbacks to the chocolate bar scenarios when I hear this dubious reasoning.

If the word *balance* was used to mean an equitable sharing of resources, landscapes or chocolate, it would be easier to swallow. The reality is that most of our landscapes and natural resources have already been developed, changed or in some way lost. If we have already converted 80 per cent of the natural world into some economic endeavour, it is disingenuous to claim that we are achieving balance as the remaining 20 per cent is carved up. We are not weighing two equal things.

The word balance is a changeling, depending on who is using it. When off-highway vehicle lobbyists say, "Yes, the environment is important, but we must find a balance," they usually mean, "We want to continue to drive off-road with a minimum of restriction." Loggers say it's important to balance protection of old-growth forest with forest renewal through clear-cutting. What they really mean is, "Keep the annual allowable cut high for better economic return." The oil patch says we need a balanced approach to the control of greenhouse gas emissions because the proposed actions would cost too much. In other words, "Action on reducing Earth's temperature is aspirational."

Politicians talk of "balancing responsible resource development with the needs of our diverse landscapes." Only they could combine two plastic words – "balance" and "responsible" – into a fog of bureaucratic bafflegab.

Without a starting point (a benchmark in time from which to measure), trend analysis and a sense of thresholds and limits, balance is a meaningless term. Instead of giving us direction for resource management, it sets the stage for continuing to divide up the spoils (like nibbling away at the chocolate bar) until the bits that are left are not worth fighting over. It avoids all that uncomfortable argument about resource depletion, loss of biodiversity and ecosystem failure and encourages us to think the status quo can continue.

In government planning, I have noted a tendency to ignore everything that happened prior to the plan and allocate resources based on what's left. Institutional amnesia magically erases the existing development footprint, allowing further division to be made, as we continually add to the imbalance of future development against protection. And, as the imbalance grows, we are further separated from the environment that sustains and provides for us.

Balance sounds appropriate, as any smooth-sounding word does, but it allows considerable room for manipulation and misunderstanding. Listen for the word in the centrifugal rhetoric of public relations messaging. The hidden meaning of balance seems to be excessive, unequal division and use of resources, not an equitable sharing, proportional use or restraint. Balance has to convey something more than two wolves and a sheep voting on what to have for dinner.

Life balances itself on a precarious ledge; through our actions we can nurture it or propel it off the edge. Cultivating too close to a stream, for example, removes most of the vegetation that provides natural water filtration, an essential ecosystem function. Frogs, fish, dragonflies and other aquatic creatures then suffocate under a deluge of mud, causing a cataract of consequences within the entire riverine system. Downstream, water treatment costs escalate.

To restore function and wild creatures, a drastic rebalance is necessary. That means rolling back the tide of development in a fine adjustment between giving and taking. Imagine the thorns and thistles of local resistance and business opposition to *that* idea of balance!

So how much is enough? Ecologists like the world-renowned E.O. Wilson have long insisted that "Nature needs half." We need to protect and maintain half of the landscape to maintain ecosystem functions – just for our species to survive. Of course, much of the world's biodiversity would ride our coattails on this one.

I suggest we use the term balance as you might for your bank account. Too many withdrawals – too many expenses and not enough income – means we are going broke. Calculations from the Worldwatch Institute indicate that the planet has about 1.9 hectares of biologically productive land per person to supply resources and absorb wastes. Yet the average person on Earth already uses 2.3 hectares worth, with massive global inequity. The average American uses more than 20 times the number of hectares of the average Mozambican. That's one signal we're overextended, especially in the Western world.

A report prepared by 1,360 scientists for the World Bank warns that about two-thirds of the natural machinery that supports life on Earth is being degraded by human pressure. Dr. Bill Rees, the originator of the "ecological footprint analysis," calculates that we in the Western world are using the equivalent of about two and a half Earths to meet our demands.

Of course, there are no extra Earths, and this suggests we have failed to balance our ecological chequebooks. It is ironic that those most obsessed with the idea that governments need to eliminate deficit spending in the economy continue to promote it in the environment.

Victor Hugo, the famous 19th-century writer, remarked that "to put everything in balance is good, to put everything in harmony is better." Harmony implies restraint, stewardship and sustainability. To that end, we have to decide between what we want and what we need. A gulf exists between these two points, in part because of the blind use of the word "balance." We can fall into the deadly trap of thinking that balance implies we need not concern ourselves with limits and can therefore carry on with this ecological Ponzi scheme forever.

When the word balance is used, look for imbalance instead. Instead of acts of self-restraint, "balancing" competing demands liberates us from the tough decisions of limits. Writer and conservationist Kevin Van Tighem, obviously fed up with this word and how it is manipulated, has suggested a moratorium on its use.

In the end, we must recognize that we can't have it all, that because we've taken too much, some needs to be given back. I should have told my brother that, as he was dividing up the chocolate bar!

THE SAGA OF "ED" THE DUCK, AND OTHERS

In the movie *On Golden Pond*, Henry Fonda's character pursues a big trout named Walter. Walter the fish apparently had a personality, and it gave Fonda's character meaning, if a fish can perform such a miracle. Their bond, and the dynamic tension between them, is poignant.

In a strange turn of events, Walter reappeared, or was reincarnated, as a large rainbow trout named Gus, who was marooned in a water-filled construction hole on the grounds of the Sam Livingston Fish Hatchery in Calgary. Work progressed around Gus on an outdoor interpretive display for the Bow Habitat Station along the banks of the Bow River. Workmen routinely checked to ensure that the trout was still occupying the deep puddle. Care was taken not to muddy the water or to disturb Gus during construction. As an unintentional interpretive display and awareness program, Gus succeeded beyond the best of planned initiatives.

Then there was the mallard drake in the Inglewood Bird Sanctuary in Calgary with a plastic six-pack holder firmly gripping his green head. He became Ed the Duck, probably linked to a British puppet mallard with a ham allergy. Whether Calgary's Ed was allergic to ham was never determined, but he remained stubbornly averse to capture. His fate captivated various print and screen media in Calgary (and much of southern Alberta) for almost two weeks. The nightly TV news had updates on attempts to capture Ed and liberate him from his human-induced dilemma. Even the national news covered this wildlife drama.

As Ed continued to elude capture, the emotional outpouring from well-meaning people ratcheted up. Finally, one individual dove off a footbridge Rambo-style (breaking his leg in the process) and "rescued" Ed. Wildlife rarely gets that much exposure in the media, but Ed, with his plastic six-pack collar, managed it in spades.

As a biologist I'm not immune to the allure of wild individuals. On an Earth Day drive a few years ago, to watch the timeless return of waterfowl to prairie wetlands, my wife and I found a short-eared owl impaled on a barbed wire fence. Short-eared owls are not rare, and saving this one would not make a difference one way or the other to the grassland population of the species. That never entered our minds. We carefully extracted it from the barb and rushed it to a wildlife rehabilitation centre some distance away. There, we expressed our concern and offered a hefty donation to ensure that it received veterinary and extended care. When we found a postcard in the mail many months later with news of its successful convalescence and release, we were thrilled.

The issue with that short-eared owl and its kin speaks to the loss of native grasslands and the fragmentation of the landscape with fences, which in this case snared the unsuspecting owl as it went about its business. When Aldo Leopold suggested "thinking like a mountain," he meant considering the needs of the whole wildlife community (and landscape integrity) rather than those of one individual, alone.

In all of the coverage of Ed the Duck, not once was the loss of waterfowl habitat, especially the pervasive loss of prairie wetlands, ever discussed. Gus the rainbow trout never got his message across that many rivers, or river reaches, in southern Alberta can no longer function as habitat for trout, let alone for any fish, because of diversions for irrigation agriculture. Nor did he have the opportunity to lobby on behalf of his wild cousins, the bull trout and the Westslope cutthroat trout, imperilled because of land uses like logging and roading.

It is one thing to see an individual bird (or any species of wildlife or fish), to watch it, to identify its characteristics and to name the species. It is a far bigger step to realize what that individual embodies – energetics, migration, interactions, habits and habitats, population dynamics, and threats. Naming something like a bird is generally done to make it familiar or notable – to capture the individual in one's memory. Until we can see through the bird to all the factors that make and maintain a bird, a bird is all we see.

The challenge is to distinguish between caring for the good of a species and obsessing about an individual creature. Picture a nonhuman animal: the bright eyes, the sleekness of feathers or fur, the fierce independence, the wildness. Everything else disappears, sometimes even the bars on the cage. Whether it's a photograph or a flesh-and-blood sighting, what jumps into focus is the animal. The background, the population, the connections and the habitat are out of focus, out of mind and largely unseen.

The basic unit of biodiversity is not the individual but the population of which that animal or plant is a part. An individual is but a comma in the sentence that is the population. A population should be thought of as the reproductive community that keeps turning out workable individuals. Evolution's raw material is not the individual but the population whose pool of genes provides robustness and is the intermediary between today's individual and the future survival of the population.

While it seems harsh, individuals are, in the greater scheme of things, expendable. It is the population, the collection of individuals, that must meet the rigours of natural selection over space and time. Focusing on the individual, cute or fierce or iconic as the animal might be, is like tuning to the wrong channel; context is the only one that counts.

It's the herd, the flock, the school and the grove that matters. Our responsibility is to species, not specimens; to communities, not individuals; to populations, not single creatures.

A fixation on the individual does little to connect the essential dots. It might be dangerous to overinvest individual animals with symbolism. Who can resist the yawn of a lion, a timber wolf howling on a snowy ridge, or a dappled whitetail deer fawn nestled in tall grass? But unless we connect that lion, wolf or deer to place, the place may not remain to sustain the individual.

Habitat is where species occur, reproduce and thrive. Habitat is the foundation for the existence and persistence of species.

Wildlife embody the landscape in which they survive. A focus on the landscape, including the human footprint, provides a lesson on adaptability, connectivity and resilience. It's the habitat, not the individual, that defines the persistence of wildlife and our ability to interact, enjoy and learn from them.

In conservation, the most powerful, evocative message is about consequences and what is at stake for wildlife to persist. A deeper appreciation is, inevitably, what connects us and helps us realize that we are of the same world and circumstance. "One touch of nature makes the whole world kin," said the wise bard, William Shakespeare.

To see wildlife as fellow creatures – to care, to envision a future for them as well as ourselves – requires the acquisition of a sense of context. It calls for balancing the emotion related to the individual with pragmatism about the population and its habitat.

Wild animals are not named Woody, or Smokey or Pooh, nor do they live a happy-go-lucky, magical life at Disneyland playing a ukulele for the tourists. They don't exist solely in a National Geographic special, or as the emblem of an insurance company, a trucking firm or a country.

The development of empathy for wildlife does not rest with making animals more human, by transforming them into patriotic symbols or exploiting them as a kind of wilderness porn. It lies in recognizing that Ed the Duck and other individuals do not stand alone. All wildlife creatures share a common landscape with us; their presence can be a metric showing how well we can manage that place, and their disappearance should alarm us.

The rest is just unconnected distraction, tinged with shallow entertainment.

BRAKING FOR THE PLANET
Learning the Limits

It would have been the wildest hyperbole to have called my father a patient teacher, especially in coaching someone to drive a car. Had my mother not enrolled me in a driver training course, I would still be a pedestrian.

There, under the tutelage of a very patient instructor, I learned many important driving tips, not the least of which was the idea that stop signs meant *Stop!* They were not yield signs to motor through when the traffic seemed light. Another was the concept of leaving a suitable distance between yourself and other moving vehicles to allow for safe stops. I wasn't to realize until much later what a grounding in ecology these fundamental driving tips were.

Technology has gotten in the way of good driving skills. Cruise control, a standard feature on most modern vehicles, is a servo-mechanism that takes over the throttle of the car to maintain a steady speed as set by the driver. It is a curious bit of technology, at least as far as most of us use it.

Watch, on any highway, as drivers with their cruise control engaged are reluctant to disengage it when approaching another vehicle or when entering a curve or an area of traffic congestion. Cruise control can be disengaged with the flick of a finger, yet the tendency is to keep the speed up, despite looming danger. Brake lights flash at the last possible moment. Failure to disengage in a timely way can lead to unsafe and dangerous responses, collision, and death.

This is resource use on autopilot – mind unengaged, attention unquestioning. It is using things up at a speed that isn't safe, hoping we can steer around the issues coming up much too quickly in front of our grill. Rather than cruise control, it really is cruising with little or no control. It may be a metaphor for our overconsumptive lifestyle.

Braking for the planet before the planet breaks is essential. Fundamental to this is the reality of finite limits to space, resources and energy. This is couched in a variety of terms. A "tipping point" happens when a small shift in pressure or condition occurs that brings about a large, often abrupt change in a system. It is synonymous with "threshold," the point after which an ecosystem may no longer be able to return to its previous state because its resilience is too compromised. Think of a threshold as a stop sign. There are also "regulatory limits," points in some variable up to which a risk of system change is permitted (as in legislation or policy) or accepted (as in social or economic values).

What are some safe speeds for resource use? What are the limits, and where should we stop?

Until a certain point is reached, populations, habitats and ecosystems have the ability to bounce back from pressures and stressors. When a rubber band is stretched too much, elasticity is lost, a snap occurs, and the ability to rebound back to a robust form is lost. Similarly, nonhuman Nature can be pushed beyond its considerable resilience. As Aldo Leopold observed, "All ecology is replete with laws which begin to operate at a threshold and cease operating at a ceiling."

The change may be dramatic, like a light switched off. Fish disappear with a chemical pollutant above a certain concentration, a swift change in water chemistry, an increase in water temperature, or the drying up of a stream due to drought or irrigation diversions.

The change might be less dramatic and more gradual, like a dimmer switch, where a population declines on a gradient until the light of resilience goes out. Fish and wildlife populations require a critical mass, a minimum number of viable individuals, to maintain themselves. For a long time, this was the concern with whooping cranes – not enough nesting pairs.

The idea of critical mass is expressed as the smallest number of individuals in a population capable of persisting over time without winking out from natural and human causes. Once the numbers drop below the point, the chances of successful reproduction to fill the void are overwhelmed by additive mortality (factors that cause an immediate reduction in survival), changes in suitable habitat conditions, and/or competition with introduced species. The end happens not with a bang but with a whimper.

Research points out that a major army of ecological disruption and destruction comes by road. For many species, the cause of their declines is too much human traffic and its associated disturbance.

Recent University of Alberta research on the relationship between roads and grizzly bears found that areas with road densities (length of road in a given area) greater than 0.6 km/km² had lower bear populations compared with areas with less road density. Clayton Lamb, the principal researcher, summarized the work thusly: "Not only do bears die near roads, bears also avoid these areas, making many habitats with roads through them less effective."

Roads and native trout don't mix well either. All linear features – roads, trails, pipelines, skid trails and the like – intercept runoff, capturing it and redirecting it downhill. The resulting faster runoff increases erosion along the way and then dumps excess water and sediment into watercourses, to the eventual dismay of trout.

Fisheries biologists generally agree that the best road density to protect trout is zero roads/km². Where linear density has been calculated for the Eastern Slopes, it exceeds 2.0 km/km² and is, in some areas, as high as 5.0 km/km². In stark terms, the best available science shows that native trout populations can be expected to decline beginning with the first road in a watershed.

Prairie grasslands and many of the bird species that nest there are not immune to human footprints. A growing body of research has noted deleterious effects from noise, well density, conversion of native grassland, vehicle traffic and human activity. Impacts on sensitive species become apparent at low levels of disturbance, even when as little as 3 per cent of the landscape is disturbed. As researcher Jason Unruh points out: "These are not large-scale disturbance factors yet they still have detectable effects on grassland songbird abundance."

Given current rates of greenhouse gas emissions, the overall global temperature is projected to rise 1.5 degrees Celsius between 2030 and the early 2050s, according to climate change experts. Doesn't sound like much; an insignificant threshold. But with that temperature increase comes the real risk of tipping points for the melting of Arctic sea ice and the Greenland and Antarctic ice sheets.

Melting ice causes a rise in sea levels, a rise that may reach as much as a metre above current levels by 2100, according to the Intergovernmental Panel on Climate Change. Again this seems insignificant, except for people living on ocean coasts. Currently the storm surge risk for New York City is once every hundred years. With a one-metre rise in sea level, the storm surge risk for the city changes to once every three to four years, which is hardly insignificant.

A threshold is a line drawn in the sand, a boundary that science says is a stop sign. It's a cliff edge or a border, not to be breached without consequences and repercussions. But the line seems so tenuous, innocuous or unbelievable that we cross it and redraw it a little further on to allow another wellsite, road or cutblock, or another degree of warming. Once we're accustomed to crossing the line, it gets easier to redraw it again and again, for it seems that nothing catastrophic happens when it's crossed. And often nothing does, initially. Too late, the effects become too clear to be ignored.

We are at a time where too many wants compete with limits. Because we don't want to think about or engage in limits, the number of consequences and complications escalate. It seems easier to dream than to unseat a culture drunk on the illusion of plenty, impatient with restrictions, determined to wring more from a landscape than can be done sustainably.

A rancher friend whose livelihood depends on understanding limits pointed out, "You can't put more grass on your Visa card if you've overgrazed your land." He looks at the large clear-cuts next to his grazing lease and wonders how this could ever be called "sustainable" forest management.

Our lives should provide guidance, since they include speed limits (which would reduce injury and death if we adhered to them), spending limits (but credit card debt is at an all-time high), eating limits (obesity is a growing problem), drinking limits (impaired driving is still a concern) and physical limits (yet we engage in little exercise). So it's no surprise that land-use limits continue to be ignored.

Cruise control for our cars was an invention that has made us lazy and complacent in our driving habits. Ignoring or avoiding ecological limits has had a similar effect on our decision-making function for appropriate amounts of land and resource use. New cars with advanced safety systems to help avoid or mitigate collisions are already on the market. Imagine if we applied similar collision-avoidance technology to the landscape to help us avoid approaching or crossing essential ecological thresholds.

It isn't the technology we need, though; it's the discipline of setting and maintaining limits on our activity. This would represent a shift from "How much can we grab?" to "How much should we leave?" If the current overexploitive tendencies persist, we will continue to use science and technology to press harder on the gas pedal and not on the brakes.

How hard can it be to apply the brakes? Perhaps, if we learn to use the brakes, the next step will be to shift into reverse and begin the task of restoring the places where we've exceeded the limits. Already there are examples of efforts to revegetate stream banks with willows to restore riparian functions, replant old cultivated fields with native grasses, and block old roads and trails to traffic to allow natural regeneration to occur.

My driving instructor instilled in me the concept of defensive driving – being observant and engaged and understanding limits. It isn't a large leap to apply these principles to how we manage ourselves, our needs and the future of the planet.

A DANGEROUS MAN WITH A DANGEROUS CONCEPT
Cumulative Effects

———

Once, in a far-off land in another time, a ruler had a vision of an impending famine. To prepare for this contingency, he bought up all the grain in the surrounding area to feed his subjects. The famine came to pass, his subjects had enough to eat, but he discovered too late that the grain was contaminated and those who ate it went mad. The ruler summoned his most loyal subject and gave him all the uncontaminated grain that existed. He admonished him to eat only that grain. "Why me?" asked the loyal subject. The ruler considered the question and answered, "Because you are young, and we will need someone sane, when we are all mad, to tell us what we are."

In present times, many have eaten from the mythical tree of constant growth, inevitable progress and inexorable economic advancement to the point of madness. To hold up a mirror, "to tell us what we are" and to inject some sanity in a growth-focused world is a dangerous yet necessary undertaking.

Over time there have been some notably dangerous men and women who have toppled conventional thinking, confronted the status quo, debunked ideologies and pried the blinders off politicians and the rest of us. Copernicus and Darwin come to mind. In a contemporary way, some of the Davids taking on the Goliaths of industry, commerce, politics and entrenched self-interest have included David Suzuki, David Schindler and Rachel Carson.

You would not consider someone of medium height, with an innocent face and wispy, barely controlled blonde hair, who is usually clan in jeans and a barely tucked-in shirt, to be a dangerous man. But to many in the corporate and political world, Dr. Brad Stelfox is one of those who, in the parlance of the 1960s, questions authority. He does it in an uncharacteristically subversive way, using data from industry, government and academia.

The tool used to question our growth assumptions is called cumulative effects assessment, or CEA. Using years of data, Brad developed ALCES (A Landscape Cumulative Effects Simulator) to objectively measure and track land-use activities and their accumulating footprint. With this tool, Brad can model the future.

We all talk about the future, maybe even believe there is one, but most of us tend to think and act in the here and now. That's why it is always a surprise when we run short of clean water, land, space and wildlife. It's hard to add up the incremental changes and losses, do the math over time, and project that trend line into the future. When the future catches up with our present, we are deeply shocked – even mortified – with the limitations of our world.

That's the mirror Brad holds up, showing that our world isn't limitless and our growth trajectory isn't endless. This is the part that doesn't endear him to some. We tend to see the world in snapshots – one wellsite, another subdivision, a new road, or more prairie cultivated. We lack the skill to do the additive math of all these features transforming the landscape. Our memories are also imperfect about when all of these features snuck up on us – "When did the neighbour build that garage?" or "I thought there used to be a wetland here."

All effects, all land uses, are cumulative simply because everything accumulates and lingers both through time and over space. In a "tyranny of small decisions," a series of seemingly individual and insignificant changes can accumulate to result in a consequential effect overall. The cumulative effect of stressors can be more than the simple sum of individual ones. It might be akin to learning of a threatening medical diagnosis, having a flat tire, losing one's job and undergoing a marital breakup – all at once.

It becomes seductively easy to believe that the way things are is the way they were meant to be and always will be. Such thoughtlessness leads to blindness. Unless we claw the security blanket of growth from our eyes, it will prevent us from recognizing the truth of our situation – that we are walking a tightrope without a safety net. We remain fundamentally, inexorably dependent on intact natural systems with a high degree of integrity for our survival.

While we live in the present, we are affected by the past and inevitably head into the future. It would be of considerable comfort to know what the future brings. Rather than passively wait for it, we can invoke choice rather than chance. We can direct the future with wise decisions today. CEA is one of the very few tools that gives us the capability to understand today's actions and their implications for tomorrow. If we wish to move forward intelligently, this tool can inform the pathway into the fog of the future.

We all yearn to divine the future, to understand what it has in store for us. For most things that is a dream – the realm of fortune tellers or fortune cookies. As Brad shows, the past can be a window on the future, if we organize, systematically analyze and strategically use existing information.

The process of modelling cumulative effects neither defends nor demonizes the status quo, often termed the "business as usual" case. As Brad says, "While there may be no inherent right or wrong in our decisions, there inevitably will be consequences."

Even though we build it every day, the future eludes us. The greatest discovery in each generation is that we can alter the future by changing what we do today. The ability to simulate future circumstances based on established trends isn't perfect, but it beats guessing and it gives form to imagination. We need tools like this to make appropriate choices rather than relying on coin tosses or dartboards to define the future.

Visions of the future can be unpopular because listeners perceive that they will be affected in a negative way. Understanding what the future may bring introduces an aspect of change, from the familiar and expected to the new and uncertain. Those who want to do nothing and make no change can find enough uncertainty to avoid doing anything. Cumulative effects models can deal with skepticism but not denial. The point of CEA is to inform change while change is still possible and to exercise flexibility, alternatives and choice.

Brad is the first to acknowledge that the science of CEA cannot give us all the answers. In fact, the most difficult questions, the most persistent problems and the greatest challenges are often not matters of science. They are related to values. It would seem that the primary impediment to resource stewardship is not a lack of evolutionary or ecological understandings. It is more often related to social, political and economic factors. The problem is not that we do not know enough, but that we do not allow what we know to constrain our behaviour.

Cumulative effects assessment can tell us what is happening and is likely to happen, but it cannot make us do anything about it. The utility of CEA lies in seeking agreement on what future is desired and then moving towards that future, not through guesswork but through the tools of science, which include thought, planning and foresight.

Douglas Chadwick observed about these tools that "all are part of the challenge of learning as a modern society how to live the good life on earth without abusing the generosity of our hostess." The work that Brad undertook to develop a method for measuring and tracking cumulative effects helps us with that challenge, dangerous as it might seem to some.

2

The Tiny, the Cryptic
and the Overlooked

The beauty of the natural world lies in the details.

— Natalie Angier

THE BEAVER
An Ally or an Inconvenient Species?

———

The beaver is quite a package. They swim like a fish, cut wood like a chainsaw and move materials like a front-end loader. Beavers are the first water engineers and the first loggers, transforming landscapes at a scale that rivals the efforts of humans. Some might consider beaver an inconvenient species.

Despite being our national symbol, the beaver is equally loved and hated and is universally misunderstood. Beavers seem to come with either horns or halos. When they flood roads and property, cut favourite trees or make an apparent mess of a beloved stretch of river, they can seem to be evil incarnate. But to the myriad plant, insect, fish and wildlife species for which beaver create habitat, and to those who appreciate fishing, birdwatching and Nature generally, beavers are divinely inspired. Most importantly, they are seriously underrated in terms of their contribution to maintaining biodiversity, restoring stream function and helping us weather the gathering storm of climate change.

The essence of climate change (or climate chaos, as it is sometimes called) is greater variability in our weather. For many landscapes, the trend is towards warmer and drier conditions. Climate change also brings more violent storms that dump massive amounts of rain in a short time period. It's a conundrum of less precipitation overall, but with faster delivery than the landscape can absorb. In a perverse way, it means increased drought and flood conditions, often within the same year.

What beavers do, and have done for centuries, can mitigate some of this increased variability. We may have overlooked a natural ally in our efforts to conserve and manage water, as well as moderate risk.

Beavers and their activities seeped into my psyche during the droughts of the 1980s. With streams drying up, ranchers contacted me to see how to rebuild old beaver dams so as to provide reliable water for their cattle. One rancher, who had wisely protected his beaver population, resisted all efforts to blow up the dams to allow a trickle of water to pass downstream, knowing the feeble stream would quickly disappear into the gravel.

When beavers hear running water, it clicks the switch into dam-building mode. Deeper water is a safer home for beaver. Beaver dams create impoundments of stored water, often of significant volume. Dr. Glynnis Hood, the acclaimed beaver researcher from the University of Alberta, found that ponds with resident beavers in Elk Island National Park had nine times more open water than those without beavers. Beaver activity can increase the amount of open water in a watershed by nearly 10 per cent, according to other research.

But that's only the water we can see. Beneath the ponds and adjacent areas is a much more profound story. Some speculate that the amount of hidden groundwater storage is three to ten times the volume of water behind the dam. The actual amount of water is variable, depending on the storage capacity of subsurface materials. Dr. Cherie Westbrook, from the University of Saskatchewan, has found that beaver activity routinely raises the groundwater table and maintains it, even in drought conditions.

Beaver ponds both store and deliver water. By slowing water down, allowing it to seep into shallow aquifers, beaver activity increases downstream flows from two to ten times more than streams without beavers. Most importantly, that water is delivered later in the season, when flows are normally low (and in drought, very low), helping fish survive and providing essential supplies to us downstream water drinkers. Beavers keep wetlands wet and streams flowing.

One of the wicked problems of climate change is larger and more prevalent wildfires. Fortuitously, the saturated soils and wet patches created by beavers in dry areas create fire breaks, slowing the speed and extent of wildfires.

On another front, beaver dams function as speed bumps for streams, decreasing the velocity of moving water. Moving water has incredible power, especially during floods, and can be extremely destructive. An array of beaver dams and ponds in a watershed can delay and reduce the flood peak and the energy associated with that quickly moving mass of water.

Beaver dams also increase the width of the effective flood plain up to 12 times. Wider flood plains work to slow down water by spreading it out. This reduces the erosive force, allowing water to be captured in surface irregularities and eventually some seeping into shallow aquifers. Much of the sediment carried by flood waters is dropped on the flood plain, improving water quality. In short, beaver dams result in the impact of a flood being dampened, slowed and reduced, which decreases the negative impacts on downstream communities.

Our very costly attempts to mitigate floods and droughts aren't always successful. Engineered structures often destroy many natural attributes, negatively affect fish and wildlife populations, and detract from the beauty of natural landscapes. Yet human engineers seem reluctant to accept the help of beavers in moderating floods.

More beaver dams and ponds in watersheds would increase the capacity to capture and tame flood flows, mitigate drought and better manage risk. Integrating the beaver into our future flood, drought and watershed plans would reduce costs and negative impacts and add substantial benefits.

These natural dam builders and water engineers can be aggravating and helpful, costly and beneficial. Because Cows & Fish (a.k.a. the Alberta Riparian Habitat Management Society) covers all things riparian, the organization educates and helps people live with beavers. It is a matter of the right time and place, some mitigative tools, and a healthy dose of tolerance and knowledge.

The challenge is that current beaver populations are a fraction of historical numbers. Population recovery has been slow, partly because we have not fully understood and appreciated the many services provided by beavers that benefit us. A careful look at the beaver shows that it is a most convenient species to have as an ally as we adjust to water scarcity and periodic water overabundance.

HARE-FOOTED LOCOWEED

Amid the melting snow, a hardy survivor of storms and droughts and ice sheets pokes its tentative blossoms towards the prairie sky.

Cloaked in a sensible woolly coat, it defies the extremes of its home. At its peak, the plant stands only as tall as your fist. If you are searching the prairie sky for signs of spring, you will miss it, since its ground-hugging nature requires a discerning and trained eye to locate it. It blooms early, sets seed quickly and retires to a quiescent existence for the rest of the year.

Rodents, ground squirrels and the hares that the plant is named after (the fuzzy sepals resemble a hare or rabbit's foot) may pilfer some of the seeds, and an occasional cow may lop off a bit of the plant top, but the greatest danger comes from us, in the form of cultivation and gravel excavation.

It doesn't ask for much, this diminutive plant – a bit of soil amid the gravels of some long-forgotten river bottom now forming the top of the Del Bonita Plateau and the Milk River Ridge in southwestern Alberta. Along the plateau rims and steep ridges, where the soil is thinnest and the gravel most ex- posed – a place of near-constant wind and little competition from other plants – grows hare-footed locoweed.

Much of the place where it now lives was surrounded but not covered by the ice of continental glaciers in the Pleistocene epoch. Hare-footed locoweed may well have watched the receding glaciers as it established a toehold in a new, raw world. It may have welcomed the new tourists to a rapidly thawing land – bison, camels, horses, mastodons, mammoths and sabre-toothed cats. First Peoples would have travelled, camped and hunted within sight of the plant. It may have witnessed the carnage as bison were stampeded off the steep ridge lines.

Hare-footed locoweed stood mute as much of the adjacent fescue grassland was plowed up decades before we recognized the merits of intact grasslands and made fescue our provincial grass. The march of introduced plants, a legacy of cultivation, may have registered with hare-footed locoweed.

But plants don't wonder, don't speculate and don't pass judgment; they simply endure. The hare-footed locoweed has rolled each successive storm, every drought, and the vagaries and consistencies of its surroundings into its genetic memory bank. We can't know what a plant feels, and by conventional definition the hare-footed locoweed is not a sentient being . But it makes one wonder when the places it has arranged to live have such expansive, impressive views.

The stories a hare-footed locoweed could spin if it had a mind to and a voice! Of course, it might be reticent to talk to us human youngsters, with our short tenure and no experience of surviving the long haul. Maybe we haven't been around long enough to listen with intent. What would we have in common?

The plant contains an alkaloid, poisonous to livestock if too much is ingested. Alkaloid poisoning causes livestock to go "loco," hence the name locoweed. As scattered as the plant is, a cow would have to be fatally diligent to do itself in from eating hare-footed locoweed.

As far as I know, no odes have been written to hare-footed locoweed – only a dusty tome on its status for some committee whose members will probably never see the plant. Thankfully, no one will ever gather a bouquet of its bluish/purple flowers, since they are too small to attract attention. Bumblebees are attracted to the perfume of its blossoms, but for the rest of us, that subtle scent is lost to the unremitting wind.

No flock of plant aficionados will travel to admire it and revel in this muted signal of spring. There is no evidence that the plant contains a cure for some debilitating disease, although the Blackfoot apparently chewed it to alleviate sore throats.

We might think it unimportant, just another nondescript plant with a strange Latin name. It's the way we tend to treat all the uncharismatic microfauna and flora – of no particular interest, ignored and soon forgotten. Hare-footed locoweed plucks no heartstrings, except of those who know the world is made of many parts, all of which have purpose and none of which are superfluous.

Maybe we can grasp, even in some fundamental way, that a hare-footed locoweed clinging to the edge of a coulee rim is a metaphor for our own dependence on one lonely orb in outer space.

KISSING FROGS
A Tale of Stewardship

In the Brothers Grimm fairy tale "The Frog Prince," a royal son is bewitched and transformed into a frog by a wicked witch. The kindness of a princess (which in one version of the tale involves a kiss) allows him to be returned to his human form. And then they live happily ever after.

If only the plight of northern leopard frogs in Alberta were so easily fixed. With dramatic declines in numbers and only 30 known breeding sites in the province, these frogs need help. Can stewardship be part of the solution across Alberta? Kris Kendell, with the Alberta Conservation Association (ACA), thinks it can: "Watching tadpoles develop, catching frogs, or being serenaded by a chorus of frog music captivates many of us," he says. "Working with hundreds of rural landowners is essential to amphibian [and other wildlife] conservation. We need landowners and we can help them with their stewardship efforts."

One family, the Balogs, on their ranch in southern Alberta, provides some insights into how it can be done. They haven't kissed any frogs, but their stewardship efforts have allowed the frogs on their land to survive and thrive. What was it about the northern leopard frogs that evoked empathy and responsibility for them? It's clear the Balog family values these frogs and willingly shares the ranch with them. Stewardship can be a complex decision to explain, but it's easy to observe.

As Ken, the fourth generation of the family on the ranch, says, "If frogs aren't thriving around the dugout and along the creek it says something about our management. Maybe we have done some things right, because the frogs are still here. But can we do things better?"

The spark to start that process of doing things differently often occurs in a conversation over a cup of coffee. The Balogs have always taken a keen interest in the wildlife that flies over, walks across or swims through the ranch. It's part of an interest in all aspects of the ranch – part of being "watchers." But from time to time, even the keenest of watchers needs some outside help, as the Balogs discovered. Although they were aware of frogs, it wasn't until a pair of biologists sat down at the kitchen table to explain the results of an inventory of amphibians that it became clear that their frogs were of the threatened northern leopard variety.

Aldo Leopold, a wise ecologist and observer of people, once remarked, "Nothing so important as an ethic is ever 'written.'" Rather, it develops "in the minds of a thinking community." Making a difference is based on knowing a difference can be made; the first step along the path is awareness. With the Balogs, once they knew a threatened frog lived on their ranch, awareness translated into responsibility.

Ken and Nora have been active volunteers in their community for many years. Stewardship, a form of volunteer activity, isn't a big step for the family, and it includes caring for uncharismatic microfauna like frogs.

Stewardship of northern leopard frogs on the Balog Ranch began as, and continues to be, a productive partnership among the Balog family, ACA, and MULTISAR (Multiple Species at Risk).

The Balog Ranch lies in an arid landscape, so riparian areas, the green ribbons next to streams and around wetlands, are key for livestock management. Because they provide a reliable and easily accessible source of water, they are a magnet for livestock and wildlife. They are also incredibly productive and are critical for frogs to thrive.

Based on range inventories and a long history of grazing, the Balogs understand the long-term carrying capacity of their pastures. They also know that the theoretical "average" amount of forage may not be available in dry years, and so they adjust the annual stocking rate to compensate for rainfall variability. To both harvest forage and allow grass to recover, they rotate cattle through their pastures. There is as much art in livestock management as there is science; it is a balance tempered with knowledge and wisdom. An additional challenge comes along when the needs of frogs are added to the equation.

To learn how to factor frogs into the mix of grazing, the Balogs listened intently to the biologists' ideas. It became evident that this would not involve a loss of grazing capacity; they simply had to learn to manage livestock with the needs of frogs in mind. Frogs, like cows, thrive with clean water, lush vegetation and security for the rearing of young. Cows can linger too long in riparian areas, fouling the water and trampling critical frog habitat into mud.

It is said that riparian grazing management is simply outsmarting a cow. But maybe it's not so much about outwitting them as giving them options that take pressure off riparian areas. To maintain and enhance frog habitat, the Balogs had to manage when and where cattle would graze and for how long.

With the help of ACA and MULTISAR, they installed two off-stream water troughs to give cows an alternative to drinking directly from the stream. One system taps water from a dugout; the other is portable and allows livestock pressure points to be minimized along Red Creek. In dry years, the watering systems conserve water, a significant benefit to cows and frogs in an arid landscape.

The off-stream water sources, along with movement of salt blocks, allow for better management of cattle distribution, and that benefits both livestock and frogs. As Ken and Nora have observed, "Give cattle a choice of clean water, and they'll walk a mile to the trough." Other livestock producers have noted better weight gains with clean water. The Balogs are pleased with the health benefits to their cattle of watering sites where the animals can avoid being bogged down in mud.

There is more to this story than just better livestock management, though. The conservation and recovery of species at risk isn't magic, in a fairy-tale sense. It is the combination of pragmatic and altruistic decisions of ordinary people undertaken every day that results in a species pulled back from the brink of disappearing. And it's more, much more than moving water and salt.

It's not cows or frogs, ranchers or biologists, agriculture or environment. In this example of stewardship, there are many benefits to replacing "or" with "and." Two organizations involved in the business of conservation of landscapes and wildlife found an agricultural partner willing to work with them in the task of protecting an amphibian, the threatened northern leopard frog. Brad Downey, a biologist with ACA, observed, "We need stewards of the grassland like the Balogs. I've learned from them and I like the feeling we're working together to manage habitat for wildlife. They are real pathfinders, showing what can be done cooperatively."

The association and relationship developed between staff of ACA and MULTISAR and the Balogs went beyond strictly business. Getting to know one another over the years has led to mutual respect, credibility, learning and sharing. Another benefit was the completion of a comprehensive ranch inventory that includes range condition, grazing capability and wildlife habitats. Generated from this was a management plan to guide their efforts to maintain and sustain the ranch. Financial assistance with the off-stream water developments aided their livestock management efforts. Both cows and frogs benefited from this working relationship.

In an unanticipated way, the frogs captured the imagination of Beth, one of Ken and Nora's daughters. This was sparked by an initial school field trip to the ranch where ACA and MULTISAR biologists taught the students about frogs. From this interaction, Beth developed a fascination with frogs and later surveyed population levels along the creek. In this tale, we could say that the frog kissed the princess, not transforming her but motivating her to pursue a career path to resource management.

"I want to care." said Beth. "We all need to care about wildlife. I want to show people that even a small change can make a difference." In a way, Beth's path has led to even greater family awareness. Nora says that now "checking the cows also means checking the frogs."

As one example of stewardship, the Balogs have figured out how to live on a piece of land and maintain a species at risk. In part, it is about caring. It is also about being receptive to new ideas and to the deliverers of new ideas. The family displays the essential elements of stewardship: ecological awareness, a strong land ethic, and actions appropriate for both today and tomorrow. The harmony and relationship between humans and wildlife on the Balog Ranch is inspirational.

Like "The Frog Prince," this story too has a happy ending, for both the northern leopard frogs on the Balog Ranch and those who care for them.

OF LIZARDS, OIL AND VELCRO

———

An old Anglican hymn begins with "All things bright and beautiful, all creatures great and small." It sounds like a rousing tribute to biodiversity, and it could be if it didn't digress into religious overtones. The Christian proselytizing aside, it is a good start on a message to keep habitats "bright and beautiful" (and presumably intact) for every species "great and small."

Our actions, though, speak louder than our words when it comes to biodiversity protection. We tend to fixate on the charismatic megafauna, like grizzly bears, although even there, the reality is that we haven't done much yet to protect them. Critters in demand for hunting, fishing or viewing – like elk, rainbow trout or bighorn sheep – also get a lot of attention. But what if you suffer the misfortune to be hare-footed locoweed, or a plains spadefoot toad, or a Baird's sparrow? It's easy to fall through the cracks if you aren't a species that is visible, "useful" and numerous. Why spend time, money and energy on something of dubious value that is rarely encountered?

The answer is found in the profound words of Aldo Leopold: "To keep every cog and wheel is the first precaution of intelligent tinkering."

All species in Alberta fit into an intricate web, one we barely fathom. E.O. Wilson, the renowned ecologist, wrote, "The diversity of life forms, so numerous that we have yet to identify most of them, is the greatest wonder of this planet." So it might be considered a mark of ignorance to ask – especially of one small species, cryptically coloured and sparsely distributed – "What is it worth?"

The diminutive short-horned lizard is one such species and one of those "cogs and wheels" that Aldo Leopold advised us to keep. No doubt short-horned lizards would command more respect from us if they went on a steroid diet. As it is, they resemble, with their horns and spines, a thumb-sized stegosaurus. But this creature is not in the category of Tennyson's "Nature, red in tooth and claw." No, the short-horned lizard is more the camouflaged, concealed, inconspicuous type, going about her business out of sight and mostly out of mind of most of us.

These lizards are out of mind (and sight) for most Canadians because they eke out a living in places we don't tend to visit – like the grasslands of southeastern Alberta. This is a place universally hot and dry in summer, bitterly cold in winter, windswept in every season, and subject to more climatic variability and weather extremes than most of the Canadian prairies.

To the uninitiated, and to those without a sense of exploration, the grasslands have a hypnotically similar horizon and a scale that initially defies description. But a short-horned lizard, with eyes a couple of centimetres above the ground, probably doesn't find the view intimidating at all.

Short-horned lizards, Alberta's only lizard, are sparsely distributed throughout the grasslands in small, isolated populations. Here, they are at the northern extremity of their range, which extends to Mexico. Although long known to Indigenous Peoples, the species was described by Lewis and Clark, who collected a specimen near the mouth of the Platte River in 1804. The lizard was sent to President Jefferson, who had commissioned the Corps of Discovery Expedition. There is no record of what Jefferson thought of this prize from the grasslands of the Louisiana Purchase.

To find lizards in Alberta's grasslands, one must search the coulees and badlands, often along the edges of canyons. Be warned: if there is something harder to locate than a needle in a haystack, it is a lizard on the prairie. They don't merely blend with the background; they disappear into it with an invisibility cloak.

Look amid the junipers growing on the dark shales of the outcrops of the Bearpaw Formation, most of which extends north-northeast from the US border near Coutts in a widening tornado shape. Lizards seem to have some affinity for these shales, formed from the muddy sediments deposited by the Bearpaw Sea, part of the Western Interior Seaway that divided North America in half during the end of the Cretaceous period. In these shales are found the remains of lizard ancestors, including a species of crocodile up to 12 metres long. Today's lizards have shrunk substantially from their ancient and, mercifully for us, extinct cousin.

The diet of today's short-horned lizards has shrunk as well, to one of almost exclusively ants. Ants contain formic acid, the ultimate natural "hot" sauce. But ants don't seem to stimulate aggressive predatory behaviour in these lizards; they are "sit and wait" predators. That's probably best, since their gait can be described as a waddle, based on a flat body form atop very short legs. Despite their little legs, though, they can have home ranges up to a square kilometre, although most are much smaller.

The badlands south of Manyberries are the epicentre of Alberta's short-horned lizard populations. It is the misfortune of lizards that the area is also underlain by oil and gas. The footprint of wellsites, roads and pipelines is extensive. Although most of the lizard's habitats in Alberta are grazed by cattle, this activity seems benign. It is the industrial footprint, along with increased traffic from these developments, that is a major source of mortality.

Wellsites destroy suitable habitats, especially the juniper-dune complexes favoured by lizards. Roads and tracks left by vehicles are used as travel lanes. These turn into death traps, since it is virtually impossible to see a lizard from the cab of a truck, even if you're looking for one.

Some of this impact on short-horned lizards can be mitigated by better industrial site location, but the cumulative effect of so much activity can't be good for the health of the lizard population. A complementary issue in making the correct decisions (for lizards) on locations designated for industrial activity is an understanding of all of their habitat requirements.

Early research by the University of Calgary scientists provided a generic picture based on the places where lizards were captured. But the leap from where a creature is captured to an understanding of the total habitat picture, spatially and temporally, is long and fraught with uncertainty.

One of the nagging questions from the earlier research was, Where do lizards go in the winter? They must hibernate, but where? Knowing where these spots are, or the type of spot most likely to be used, is a crucial component in addressing a land-use referral for new industrial activity. This is especially so in winter, when no lizards can be found on the surface to signal use of an area.

Using tiny transmitters about the size of his little fingernail, Larry Powell, the University of Calgary's "lizard" researcher, took on the task of discerning the home range. Securing these transmitters to the lizards called for trial, some error, and much innovation. Tiny strips of Velcro were first glued (with surgical glue) to the lizard; an accompanying piece of Velcro was then epoxied to the transmitter. That arrangement allowed lizards, if they became snagged on vegetation, to wriggle free. In the end, though, simply gluing the transmitter to the lizard was a more workable solution and didn't harm them or impede their movements.

Initially, ten lizards waddled off into the great beyond with transmitters betraying their locations. The results confirmed some suspicions about lizard ecology, habits and habitat. Lizards live their lives mostly within an area about 60 metres in diameter. That estimation of home range helps one understand the implications of a wellsite normally 100 by 100 metres in extent. That's roughly four lizard home ranges.

Research is generally fraught with complications. Setting off into the unknown and seeking the unexpected is the adrenalin-fuelled part. Discovering flaws in design and materials that torpedo the effort is another story. In this case, the batteries in the transmitters began to fail prematurely. The secret winter spots remained, well, a secret.

A local rancher, skeptical about our ability to track something so small and slow, retorted, "Well, hell, with those little legs how far do you think they'd get?" He'd already eliminated Florida from the list of overwintering spots for short-horned lizards. Wildlife research often isn't the easiest concept to convey to the public, so community support for it is often hard-won.

Subsequent work (with better batteries and a revised timetable) added dramatically to the understanding of the secret lives of lizards. The hypothesis about overwintering sites – that lizards find natural cavities or crevices in rock outcrops as hibernacula to avoid freezing temperatures – was proven false. Their preparation for winter is much less elaborate. They hibernate in loose soil on south-facing slopes, no more than ten centimetres beneath the surface. That's not much deeper than their overall body length.

What this means is that this dinky little critter, with its somewhat comical array of spikes and horns, has evolved the ability to withstand freezing in order to survive in the prairie's extreme winter environment. Not a bad trick, and an impressive secret.

We complain over minor temperature fluctuations and tend to die if our body temperature varies more than four degrees Celsius. In contrast, short-horned lizards can survive variances that drop their body temperature from 32 degrees Celsius to below freezing. That's cool, and not only in a temperature sense.

Although research has cleared up some of the ecological mysteries of short-horned lizards, it doesn't help a biologist trying to decide on a land-use referral over a wellsite in lizard territory. All it means is that lizards could be hibernating in any place with soil conditions suitable for burrowing. That's not much to go on to create a critical winter habitat map. As the axiom goes, we cannot take care of that which we cannot see.

It's hard to envision a positive future for short-horned lizards, caught as they are in the tightening vice of ever-increasing land-use activity and decreasing government enthusiasm for biodiversity protection. The species was finally categorized as "Endangered" in 2006, after a number of years of discussion.

What this designation really means is that short-horned lizards fall into the gray netherworld of an imperilled species, where a recovery strategy takes years to plan and longer to implement. It isn't clear whether pushing lizards into a category of "Endangered" has pressured industrial development to have a lighter footprint, or no footprint at all.

With so many of Alberta's fish, wildlife and plant species on the brink, there doesn't seem to be the time or budget to monitor them all or, in many cases, to halt the slide into oblivion. The glacial speed of the process can mean a progression of "e" words, beginning with endangered and moving through extirpation to extinction.

More than two decades have passed since alarm bells for short-horned lizards started ringing. Yet a wellsite, access road or pipeline can appear almost overnight, based on a few months of planning and a short administrative period for approval.

Enter science and the advocacy of biologists within the Fish and Wildlife Division. Based on data from research on populations, a "Protective Notation" was applied in 2007 to over 16,000 acres of existing and potential short-horned lizard habitat in an area designated the Manyberries Sensitive Area. This bit of administrative colouring flags Crown lands, sending a message to industry to shift activity elsewhere or develop a more sensitive footprint. For the epicentre of short-horned lizards in Alberta this is good news.

Elsewhere, guidelines are in place that buffer habitat year-round and provide more direction to industry about avoiding harmful interactions with lizards and their habitats. One would hope this will make industry more circumspect about their activity, more cautious in planning and more sensitive in how they undertake their work. These are, however, just guidelines, with moral persuasion rather than a regulatory stick behind them.

Short-horned lizards are harmless little creatures. They don't ask for much – just a few acres of prairie badlands to call home.

If anything, they should command a little respect, with their diet of acid-laden ants, and their ability to survive freezing. Any adaptation to survive the worst the prairie can dish out seems miraculous and something worthy of more study and of protection.

Aldo Leopold admonished us with this: "The last word in ignorance is the man who says of an animal or plant: What good is it?" Short-horned lizards are part of the grasslands, and we need to keep them. That answer is sufficient.

ROUGH FESCUE
The Perpetual Motion Grass

———

The idea of something that perpetually produces more energy than it consumes is contagious and pervasive. My grandfather, an occasional inventor, was intrigued with this notion. Most of his inventions were of a pragmatic, prosaic nature: improvements in farming equipment, labour-saving devices, and new twists on old concepts. Except for one. He put a lot of work, done in secret, into an invention that, if it had worked, would have revolutionized the world.

My grandfather stares out from old black-and-white photographs with a fierce and determined look. From that look, I've deduced that my grandfather was not daunted by much. When developing one of Alberta's first rural telephone systems, he was not slowed by the lack of a brace and bit to drill through a log wall to connect a telephone. He simply shot a hole through the wall with a rifle. No sir, no trifling laws of thermodynamics would have stood in his way of developing a perpetual motion machine.

Many have dreamt of perpetual motion. There are references back to 1150 on the idea, and it still excites inventors. As an indication of the obsession over this idea and the flood of "inventions" over the centuries, the US Patent Office now has a policy of refusing to grant patents for perpetual motion machines without a working, operative model. Sadly, my grandfather never secured a patent for his work. Even he was unable to beat two of the laws of thermodynamics, simply stated as: "You can't get something for nothing," and "There is no free lunch!"

I'm not gifted in physics, but I must have some of my grandfather's fascination with perpetual motion – except mine is related to biological systems. One system, rough fescue grasslands, comes close to having the attributes of perpetual motion. Sure, these grasslands rely on an external source of energy – the sun. Yes, there is a delicate dance in the soil over nutrient requirements, and water isn't created (although it is squirrelled away and conserved).

No, we can't put a pulley on rough fescue to power a machine, or plug an extension cord into this plant to run a microwave. But it can power something more profound and precious – a self-sustaining entity that doesn't need artificial amendments, irrigation water or other accoutrements, all driven by fossil fuels. Ironically, my grandfather was never aware that the acres of rough fescue he plowed up were as close as he would come to a perpetual motion machine.

This plant, rough fescue, was once integral to the annual cycle of bison herds, especially in winter. Bison herds migrated, in a seasonal fashion, to the foothills and the central parkland to harvest the nutritious grass that cured on the stem and stood tall above snow level.

Before it encountered modern mammals, rough fescue also fed an ice age assemblage of the Pleistocene epoch – woolly mammoths, camels, giant bison, and horses, all extinct now. Grazing, periodic fire and intervals of drought were disturbances that fescue endured and built into the fabric of its ecology over more time than most of us can imagine.

It must have been something to see, the stems of rough fescue reaching up to touch the bellies of bison and elk. Millennia of the dividends of fescue growth, the litter, and the annual dead plant material fed a process of soil building to create the rich, black chernozems. The soil is dark with the accumulated centuries of humus, the decayed ancestors of current rough fescue plants. That black soil extended almost as deep as the graves of my homesteading grandparents.

Deep, fertile soils sparked the settlement of Alberta by those, like my grandparents, wanting to convert grasslands into cereal crops. The unbroken turf had never experienced this new disturbance. Like a fire, the plow "burnt" through the black soil, the "new coal" created under the fescue of the central parkland. Fertility, stored over the centuries, was squandered. In not much more than a human lifespan, most of the fescue grasslands were converted into rectangular fields.

In *The Grapes of Wrath*, a novel about the human-made ecological disaster called the Dust Bowl, John Steinbeck observed: "The land bore under iron and under iron gradually died." Sadly, we don't have a precise measurement of how much rough fescue is left in Alberta. We do know where uncultivated grasslands now occur. Unfortunately, what is lacking is the composition of the vegetation on those parcels and how much is still rough fescue. Much of our rough fescue disappeared under the iron that

Steinbeck described, especially in the central parkland, where less than 5 per cent of it remains.

Plows, large pipelines, roads, introduced plants, and intensive grazing by domestic animals can have lethal consequences. As with Humpty Dumpty, rough fescue grasslands cannot be put back together once they are ruined. Like children tearing apart a toy, we are adept at disassembling ecosystems. Sadly, except for rare exceptions, we lack the skills, knowledge and tools to reassemble or mend them in meaningful scales of space and time. Mostly, we still lack the reverence to avoid disassembling natural systems in the first place.

At small scales, often in places too dry for many other introduced plants to compete, some revegetation success has occurred. Experiments are underway using plugs, rooted seedlings painstakingly raised in greenhouse settings, to establish toeholds on ravaged industrial sites. At a cost of $1.65/ plug and a rate of one plug/m^2 (a minimal coverage), even the most math-challenged individual could calculate the cost of reclaiming an acre of rough fescue grassland. An acre of planted grassland would set you back a minimum of $7,000, but with no guarantee of success. In our increasingly economically focused world, that's a faltering step towards a valuation of intact fescue grasslands; $7,000 may be a significantly lower figure than the combined value of ecological goods, services and functions performed by healthy fescue grasslands.

Although most of the plant is bluish green, the base of the leaves is deep purple. In part for this reason, ranchers and range ecologists tag rough fescue as the "royal" grass. Pretenders to the grassland throne like Kentucky bluegrass, smooth brome, and timothy, all imports from more well-watered landscapes, sneak up valleys, draws and wet spots to establish their turf. When rain falls regularly, these species thrive and expand like the oil industry does with subsidies and weak regulations. But throw drought into the crucible, and when the shallow, easy water dries up these weaklings wilt.

In the meantime, rough fescue calmly goes about its business, prospering during drought. It has roots that penetrate deeply, up to two metres, to find water that is out of reach for the foreigners. Evolution is a test, and those that adapt survive. With rough fescue's evolutionary adaptations, productivity is less erratic, more stable, than grasslands dominated by introduced plants where production fluctuates wildly with changes in annual precipitation.

Climatologists draw on various types of evidence in determining that the droughts of the past century pale beside those encountered previously. Dr. Dave Sauchyn studies past climatic records using tree ring chronologies from ancient conifers. Some of the trees are limber pines that are over a thousand years old; these conifers are rooted in rough fescue grasslands. Maybe rough fescue plants are "old-growth" as well. Data indicates that what we think of as drought, based on our short history, the grasslands would consider a wet period. Rough fescue has been tested repeatedly – through significant, persistent intervals of little or no moisture – over a period, at least for Alberta, of over 12,000 years.

In a way, rough fescue creates its own perpetuity in the recycling of nutrients with its own growth, using its own foliage to trap, store and conserve moisture, and marshalling reserves through less-than-ideal growing conditions. When the time is ripe, it's ready to spring into flower. This gives the "royal" grass a massive leg up on other pretenders to the perpetual motion throne.

Perpetual is a long time, but rough fescue persistence starts about ten million years ago during the uplift of the Rocky Mountains and the rain shadow effects of that orogeny. Tectonic forces heaved the rocks into place, but climate and gravity shaped the landscape. To call rough fescue old is a wild understatement.

It would be imprudent for us to sacrifice rough fescue grasslands on the false altar of transitory economic development. We labour under an illusion that short-term returns from petroleum extraction, urban sprawl, cultivation, mining and linear features (like roads, pipelines and power lines) are the only things that support the economy. The merits of fescue are many, yet to the uninitiated and the uninterested, to those who believe technology and artifice will compensate, these benefits are slim – indeed, unaccountable in classic economic terms and not worth the worry. Maybe it is as Carl Sagan once observed: "A blade of grass is a commonplace on earth; it would be a miracle on Mars."

If we could build a machine that would use the energy of the sun to capture carbon dioxide (and store some of our excess carbon emissions); turn it, with the addition of water, into life-giving oxygen and the raw material (forage) for the production of red meat; and create soil, what would it be worth? Thomas Edison pointed out that "until a man duplicates a blade of grass, nature can laugh at his so-called scientific knowledge." Fescue is a miracle machine, and we don't need to invent it.

But even with rough fescue, we don't get something for nothing. Nothing is as fatal to rough fescue as indifference and inaction. It needs our recognition of its existence, our acknow-ledgement of its vital ecological (and economic) role and our commitment to quit tinkering with it. We might even beat one of the thermodynamic laws and win by keeping rough fescue grasslands healthy. We most certainly will lose if we allow them to be fragmented, invaded, plowed up, overused or paved over. So it's still evident – there is no free lunch, even with a hardy survivor like rough fescue.

Alberta has the largest area of rough fescue grassland in North America, and so we are guardians of a global treasure. To a degree, that has been recognized with the designation of rough fescue as our provincial grass. A skeptic might observe that making the grizzly bear an icon on the flag of California didn't save the bear in that state. Maybe there will be a greater chance of success with rough fescue.

Rough fescue is deep-rooted, tenacious and resilient. The plant could be a template, even a metaphor, for Alberta and an inspiration for Albertans. If we were more like rough fescue, we might treat Alberta as home, a place to live instead of a place to make a killing. It is dangerous to view native grasslands as merely untapped, unexploited resources. That's why most have disappeared.

Lyndon B. Johnson, America's 36th president and a campaigner for civil rights, social issues and the environment, once declared:

If future generations are to remember us with gratitude rather than contempt, we must leave them something more than the miracles of technology. We must leave them a glimpse of the world as it was in the beginning.

An understanding of our place in nature can be found in its basic documents. Those documents are still found in the remaining fragments of wild places, of native landscapes like rough fescue grasslands. The culture of my grandparents was one of taming and converting the raw land they found. It was also the beginning of an all-out assault on the documents telling us how to live within the limits of the land. When we destroy entire ecosystems, as we almost have with rough fescue grasslands, it is like expunging accumulated learning and wisdom from whole sections of a library.

A wise culture might appreciate that it isn't what we can take from rough fescue – it's what we can learn. Rough fescue offers lessons in humble starts and abiding patience. Francis Gardner, a rancher and a steward of fescue grasslands, completes the circle with this:

> We need to reflect and provide a reminder to our descendants [that] wealth is mostly based on soil and vegetation – the remnants of rough fescue are an echo of the endless pastures of the past. Rough fescue can show us how to persist in a place of extreme variability and do it in ways not only sustainable but perhaps even perpetual.

WHEN THE MEADOWLARK SINGS

———

The trill of a meadowlark in full song penetrated the cab of the truck, overcoming the whine of tires, radio voices and engine noise. Somehow the quality of that song, certainly not its volume, triggered a smile, and a sigh of weather-related relief.

If there is a tangible, audible signal of spring, the meadowlark produces it in an unforgettable set of notes.

"Repeated, melodious flute-like phrases" is how the Audubon Society's field guide describes the sound. Something like "Hip hip hurrah! Boys three cheers." I don't think the descriptions would help you distinguish the song of a meadowlark, but once you've heard it, the sonogram is riveted in your brain, and it signals spring.

A meadowlark's song isn't just a musical composition that gives us a sense that spring is upon us. The composition and combination of bird and song are more than that audible reminder. A meadowlark is a synecdoche, a tangible, living representation of a grassland landscape that once extended from the Rocky Mountains to the Canadian Shield and from the boreal forest to the Gulf of Mexico.

Meadowlarks return to Alberta's grassland and parkland landscapes early, to a brown world – sometimes even a white one devoid of colour. Although these birds have streaked brown upper parts, blending with the tans and browns of early spring grasslands, they harbour hidden splashes of colour. The throat and breast are a solid rich yellow, which the meadowlark males telegraph from perches on power poles, fence posts, and sagebrush clumps. Across their vibrant gold chest is an elegant black collar, resembling a black tie, as if the return is a formal event.

At one time, and not so long ago, the meadowlark's song would have signalled the return of many grassland birds. Together, the chirps, trills, twitters, whistles, buzzes, screeches, squeaks, warbles and gurgles would have been a boisterous, even raucous, cacophony of sound. The symphony of nearly 70 grassland and parkland birds, in addition to that of waterfowl and shorebirds, would have constituted a chorus of beauty and variety.

One might think that the legions of prairie explorers – David Thompson, Peter Fidler, Peter Erasmus, Anthony Henday, John Palliser, George Dawson and others – would have heard the notes and journalled about this phenomenon. They didn't. Perhaps they were more fixated on finding wildlife to eat than to listen to. John Macoun, an Irish-born botanist and bird enthusiast, collected grassland birds in Canada in 1882, but there is little mention in his notes of the riotous nature of the chorus they made. It is thought he and his companions were deaf to some of the songs and missed the subtle melodies of birds like the Sprague's pipit, which was not recorded in his bird lists.

One early traveller, the Earl of Southesk, perhaps better provisioned than most, fairly gushed over birdsong. On June 15, 1859, he wrote:

At dawn of day I was awakened by a most delicious concert of birds singing...All nature was full of cheerfulness, and the pretty songsters tuned their voices to an encouraging strain. As they fluttered around me, they seemed to beckon me forward...Sometimes one with a very deep voice would sing all alone...; then a hundred voices would answer him rapturously... and then all would unite together and chorus forth their little ditty again and again.

Sadly, where once you may have been tempted to cover your ears from the racket, there is now silence, a deficit of birdsong. The silence stems from males – whose songs are a come-on for females ("Hey baby, I've got territory with food and a great nesting spot") – being unable to find suitable habitat. No mating songs mean there are no subsequent territorial calls; no alarm, contact, flight or begging calls; and the landscape goes quiet.

This silence isn't illusory or understated. The North American Bird Conservation Initiative, in its 2019 *State of Canada's Birds*, points out the shocking statistic that 300 million birds have been lost from the grasslands since 1970. Two of every three birds have gone missing. Birds dependent on native grasslands have declined by 87 per cent. Even birds tolerant of agricultural landscapes have dropped by 39 per cent.

Aerial insectivores, birds dependent on insects for food, are suffering most of all. Not only are birds in decline, but "the little things that run the world," as ecologist E.O. Wilson describes insects, are in free fall. The finger points to agricultural alchemy – the heavy reliance on pesticides, herbicides and intensive farming. Any way you slice it, grassland birds are in sharp decline, even the "common" meadowlark.

A rite of spring passage for us is a wandering drive through the grasslands south and east of Lethbridge. It is like a tonic to see the returning birds, to realize that both they and we have survived another winter. But it is disheartening to drive down dozens of kilometres of country roads through a biological wasteland of fields covered with crop stubble and not see a single bird.

Cultivation agriculture homogenizes a landscape; most wildlife relies on vegetative diversity to meet all of their life cycle requirements. As we humans have variable tastes, so do birds. Some prefer undisturbed grassland, others require patchiness (a range of plant height and density), and a few are content with virtually bare ground. Meadowlarks like the middle ground, where the habitat is just right for them. The key to bird survival is vegetative diversity, not obliteration.

Less than 20 per cent of the historic mixed-grass prairie remains in Canada, and only a fraction of the fescue grasslands, less than 5 per cent. This loss of habitat has meant a concomitant loss of bird life. To put it into perspective, this decline in mixed-grass prairie would be like the average Canadian family with an average house size of 2,000 square feet being squeezed into one that is only 400 square feet.

Much of the remaining mixed-grass habitat is on public land (at least in Alberta), but all is subject to periodic nibbling and conversion. A quarter section (160 acres) might retain some of its native complement, but years of overgrazing, neglect and lack of oversight leave it vulnerable to sale, because it is no longer considered "valuable." It becomes a potato field, or an enlargement of an already enormous empire of wheat. In the tunnel vision and single-mindedness of economics, meadowlarks don't stand a chance against potatoes or wheat.

The goal of our spring drive is to spot the first meadowlark of spring, an icon even more representative of the season than snow geese, swans, pintails or northern shovelers. Most of these are in transit; the meadowlark is a prairie resident. Finally, after kilometres of disappointment, a male, in full-throated splendour and song, perches on an old cedar fence post beside a remnant bit of grassland, too rough to plow. Our mood improves instantaneously as the repertoire reverberates through the truck cab.

After our drive, reading an article in *Ecological Economics*, we discover that this isn't surprising. The paper reports that birds can positively influence people's moods. After analyzing data from 26,000 adults across 26 European countries, the researchers conclude that diversity in nature, especially of birds, has a great positive influence on people's moods – more so than wealth.

It's hard to curse the loss of grasslands (and birds) without being hypocritical. Both my sets of grandparents were sod-busters, and the wealth and comfort I enjoy today was made possible largely through the conversion of native landscapes to agriculture. Wallace Stegner, no stranger to grasslands, pointed out that "western history is a series of lessons in consequences."

Grassland is one of our most imperilled landscapes, and it isn't hyperbole to suggest that birds that rely on grasslands are in serious decline. We have traded the song of the meadowlark for the material pursuits of more potatoes, canola and wheat, as well as more urban sprawl and industrial sites.

In Alberta, land trusts like the Nature Conservancy of Canada and the Southern Alberta Land Trust Society – along with conservation efforts by the Alberta Conservation Association, Cows & Fish, and the Prairie Conservation Forum – have made important gains in conserving native grasslands. But the losses are still evident and development easily outpaces conservation. Endangered spaces lead to endangered species.

The diversity, abundance and distribution of birds are metrics that provide a window to understanding the health and integrity of a landscape. Results from the European Quality of Life Survey show that the sights and sounds of birds are also a major contributor to our feelings of well-being. We can't live without bread – perhaps we can't live without meadow-larks either.

Given the negative trends in grassland bird numbers, I'm not sure what audible signal subsequent generations will hear as the harbinger of spring – lawn mowers perhaps? Without birdsong, its variety and exuberance, we will surely lose an essential connection to the more-than-human world and, for anyone connecting the dots, a catastrophic loss of a big piece of that world.

It will be sad, and a failure of our stewardship, to say, as William Wordsworth did, "The things which I have seen [and heard], I now can see [and hear] no more."

3

Insights on
the Land and Us

*The real voyage of discovery consists not in
seeking new landscapes but in having new eyes.*

— Marcel Proust

"A MODEST PROPOSAL" FOR ALBERTA'S CARIBOU?

———

Caribou populations are cratering in Alberta. This should be evident even to the congenitally imperceptive among us. As we prevaricate, mumble, delay and equivocate, a day of reckoning approaches – morally, legally and financially. What do we do about caribou?

Every bureaucracy has a process for acquiring things and then for writing things off, when an inventory item is outdated, redundant, broken or lost. Such a system keeps things in balance; it's an accounting of sorts.

In hundreds of bathrooms and outdoor privies, and many offices, hangs a plaque with the pithy little saying: "The job isn't finished until the paperwork is done." Indeed!

As a competent bureaucracy, the Alberta government has forms for nearly everything, including the FIN 37. A FIN 37 allows one to write off an inventory item, squaring the books. So let's get on with finalizing the paperwork on caribou, completing the "write-off" forms, and paving the way for expanded economic activity in caribou range.

Economic moralists will tell us that to mourn the loss of caribou is just nostalgia. They would have disappeared anyway. Our lives will not be diminished with their demise. Put up a monument, with an image of a caribou in bronze. We could have a little hand-wringing ceremony at the monument's unveiling, where the champions of industry and government could wipe away a few false tears over the caribou's demise. It might seem momentarily hypocritical, but then we could get on with the important business of converting our landscapes and natural resources into tangible, fungible symbols of prosperity.

Now, lest you think I'm serious, Jonathan Swift, in 1729, wrote about a similar, seemingly intractable problem in Ireland in a pamphlet entitled *A Modest Proposal for preventing the Children of Poor People from being a Burthen to their Parents or Country, and For making them Beneficial to the Publick*, commonly referred to as *A Modest Proposal*. In it Swift suggests that the poverty-stricken Irish might ease their economic troubles by selling their surplus children as food for purchase by the richer class of society. He points out that this "will not be liable to the least objection."

Of course, the proposition to raise children to feed rich people is (and was) morally reprehensible. Swift's use of satire shone a harsh light on the stark poverty, reducing people to situations of basic survival, that existed in the Ireland of the day. Swift recognized the power of satire to rock people out of their complacency and get them mad enough to do something about a dire situation.

It is the same for many Albertans and caribou. We continue to be deluded into thinking that all our problems will have solutions – that our pace of development can continue and we can salvage some vestiges of biodiversity. We can have it all, and we simply have to wait for the technology that will allow us to erase our footprint. This is just cynical public relations to calm the environmentalists.

Our development footprint is extensive, pervasive and growing in caribou habitat. As it grows, habitat for caribou shrinks. Caribou, like most wildlife, can shift ranges, but the options are increasingly limited. Linear disturbances like roads, pipelines, power lines, and seismic trails, coupled with logged areas, reduce habitat effectiveness substantially as caribou avoid them. These features also allow predators, especially wolves, to make inroads to previously "safe" areas.

Only three of Alberta's 17 identified herds of caribou are deemed "stable," whatever the term means. Some are simply gone, even in our national parks. Most herds are plummeting, with population graphs that resemble children's slides. Herds are now largely separated from one another on diminishing islands of habitat, creating genetic isolation.

Here's where we're at: all of the work on population status indicates that caribou are in a slow race to oblivion in Alberta. Maintaining "business as usual" means the extirpation of caribou in a relatively short time frame.

How quickly will caribou leave us? It is a matter of will and choice. If enough Albertans say that caribou matter and should continue to exist, then the path is clear. We will have to surrender some of the economic engine operating in the foothills and boreal forest – or at least delay the payback period. Are we, as a civilized society with a moral and a compassionate compass, willing to forgo, delay or reduce our expectations of short-term financial return in favour of caribou and their habitat?

We need to decide, not simply delay, deny and drag out the decision. For too long, with so many species, the answer was more study, more monitoring, more stopgap measures.

As Winston Churchill observed, "When the situation was manageable it was neglected, and now that it is thoroughly out of hand we apply too late the remedies which then might have effected a cure."

Alberta has to come clean because we can't have it both ways – have our caribou and eat their habitat with industrial development too. To lose the abundance of biodiversity in Alberta, within a century of European settlement, to the demands of the corporate world (and to disconnected shareholders) is comparable to shredding all the books from every library to relieve a temporary paper shortage.

The world's doomsday clock is currently ticking at 100 seconds to midnight, signalling our potential end in a blinding flash of nuclear explosions. Caribou in Alberta are closer yet to the chiming of midnight, and if we don't stop the clock, we will have erased them after millennia of their existence.

Kirby Smith, a retired provincial wildlife biologist, with years of experience on the caribou file, relates: "On provincial lands in Alberta we've conducted the same experiment on all of the woodland caribou ranges. We've allocated all of the timber, and all of the oil and gas resources, and then acted surprised when a species that requires large areas of intact, old-growth forest consistently declines towards extirpation."

As Kirby correctly points out, half-hearted attempts to mitigate this have been made for the last 40 years, but to no avail. "The old adage of pay me now or pay me later has come home to roost and like inflation, the cost of conservation has sky-rocketed." Other biologists say it's like watching a slow-motion train wreck where few of the other watchers sense an impending disaster. For me, it goes beyond scientific objectivity to the emotion of sorrow.

A caribou is a survivor, perfectly adapted to deep snow with large, crescent-shaped hooves that act as snowshoes. A caribou does not fear deep snow; with large hooves and long legs, it floats over the stuff. Caribou subsist, over winter, on both terrestrial and arboreal lichens, themselves products of old-growth forests.

Caribou are like canaries with antlers. They are the flagship species of the boreal forest and the northern foothills, serving as sentinels marking the changes brought about by the pace and expanding footprint of our economic aspirations. Caribou declines give Alberta a failing grade for species conservation.

Death is the fate of a landscape or a creature when the effects of human impact are ignored. The future existence of caribou is a test of our commitment to maintaining the land's biodiversity. For the protection and recovery of caribou, hard but not impossible choices must be made.

Saving caribou is more than a political decision. It is a decision that corporate interests also have to make, and one in which we Albertans have to share. We are all responsible for caribou, through legislation, policy commitment and the ethics of responsible stewardship. No default to a FIN 37 is permissible.

Is rushing the remaining caribou off the provincial stage what we want recorded on Alberta's resumé? We cannot agree to write off the species, either directly or through benign neglect, any more than Jonathan Swift would have agreed to the implementation of his "Modest Proposal." At the heart of this, we are the trustees of a living being.

PRAIRIE RETURNS TO LETHBRIDGE

As they loaded up our lawn in a truck and hauled it away, my wife and I couldn't have been happier. No more watering, fertilizing, fighting dandelions, mowing and pimping up a rectangle of exotic Kentucky bluegrass for the neighbours to enjoy.

I suspect that native grasses have been absent from our Lethbridge lot for over a hundred years. Under a neighbourhood canopy of elms, spruce, birch, lilacs and other nonprairie flora, it's hard to conjure up a scene of a sun-scorched, wind-blasted, droughty grassland. But that's what it once was, and we are slowly reversing the process. At least we are to the extent of taking a postage stamp-sized front yard back to its prairie origins of being tolerant of drought.

Tony Rees, an Alberta historian, calls grasses "the plains' perfect tenants." Trees cannot compete with grass; they are here because we do not like to live without them. They have generally been transported from a more well-watered land.

Trees, wrote one pioneer, showed that "real homes" could be built on even the "bald-headed" prairie. They were a shield against prairie space, that frightful immensity of seeming nothingness. To plant a tree was to confer order and control, to have some shelter from the open grassland. On early farms, the Prairie Farm Rehabilitation Administration, the reclamation arm of the federal Department of Agriculture, felt that tree and shrub planting was necessary to ensure people stuck to their homesteads. Anything, it was thought, to make these places more attractive and appealing.

With this, and all of our clever engineering and ingenuity, most of the prairie grasslands were long ago transformed and moulded into something else to meet our economic strivings and our misplaced sense of what the landscape should look like. Perhaps it was a function of heritage. When you aren't born to prairie, there is a yearning to replicate the green, lush, shaded landscapes of a forgotten homeland. Mostly, those landscapes exist only in our dreams.

It was recognized very early in Alberta's colonial history that settling the prairies would be challenging. An 1890 editorial in the *Medicine Hat News* put it bluntly: "It would be criminal to attract people here." But the great vacant land did beckon, perhaps sparked by the colonization dreams (and lies) of the federal government and the railroad. For the last century and more, settlers and their descendants have been engaged in an unceasing endeavour to change the grassland, to make it into something else, rather than learn to appreciate its inherent qualities.

Native prairie grassland is a treasure hidden right under our feet. Grasslands are marvellously adapted, given their long evolution under arid conditions. Nothing else rivals their drought tolerance, nutrient recycling, moisture conservation capacity, resilience and ability to support wildlife. Moulded in a crucible of change for millennia, prairie grasses are tenacious and have much to teach us about adapting to our changing climate. Though their time in southern Alberta isn't deep time, the prairie grassland is at least a hundred times older than the mere century of most of our recent transformations.

What has allowed native grasses to persist over time – even through prolonged, dramatic droughts – are their deep roots. There's nothing like dry times to make a convincing evolutionary argument for seeking water at depth, where a reservoir of soil moisture exists. Native grasses send roots down metres, while the roots of exotic lawn grasses are only a few centimetres long. It also doesn't take much moisture to jump-start native grasses back from dormancy. As little as five millimetres of water – that's about four stacked dimes' worth – sparks green up.

That's a bit of background for our curious exchange of Kentucky bluegrass for native blue grama grass and other similarly drought-adapted species. What might need some more explanation is that our motivation for digging up the lawn was not only to recapture some of the past prairie history of Lethbridge but also to avoid the goofy task of mowing the lawn.

Lawn care is a necessary activity to perpetuate this alien urban landscape in the aridity of southern Alberta. It is wasteful of water, which is poured on foreign grass species that never evolved under dry conditions. Lawn care tools like gasoline-powered lawn mowers and weed whackers use fossil fuels and create greenhouse gas emissions. The end product, grass clippings, has no commercial value and, worse yet, is routinely discarded and added to landfills.

Keeping this stuff green, pristine and up to the contemporary neighbourhood standard set by lawn care experts requires routine applications of fertilizers, herbicides and pesticides. The excess chemicals run off and taint the water in our rivers and possibly the groundwater. Ironically, after all this cost, effort and impact, we spend less time on our lawns than in any other part of our homes.

The tyranny of greenery is an artifact of a different geography and economic status. In the moist, damp climate of maritime Western Europe, especially Britain, lawns grow quickly with little help from homeowners. Lawns began as pastures, common areas surrounding villages for grazing sheep and cattle. They evolved into a status symbol for the aristocracy. Before mowing machines, only the rich could afford the labour costs of managing a lawn. What these expansive lawns and parks created was an image, carried with immigrants to North America, who aspired to the middle-class dream – to own a home surrounded by green lawn.

With images of sweeping green lawns planted firmly in the imagination, newcomers to southern Alberta assumed that part of their civic duty was to maintain this anomaly despite the arid environment. It seems to be an obsession so prevalent, and pervasive, that we can't imagine anything else. It is an artifice to trick us into thinking that we live somewhere lush and green – not in a place with scant rainfall.

Our transformed front yard attracts attention. People stop and look at it, almost as if it is exotic, which it now is. Native grasslands have been reduced in scale, are dominated by introduced species, and are removed from most people's consciousness to the point where what was once native is now considered exotic.

But that's not to suggest that the blue grama grass "lawn" isn't striking in its own way. Blue grama grows close to the earth, a desirable trait in a windy, sun-drenched, dry place. What it lacks in height, it makes up for in charm. The blades roll, kink, twist and coil. Early pioneers called it "prairie wool," although the term could fit any number of low-growing native grasses that formed a dense mat over prairie soils. When blue grama goes to seed, the head resembles that of a small toothbrush. When the seed heads wave in the wind, they look like hundreds of tiny toothbrushes busily scrubbing the air.

Prairie grasses, over time (and they've had a lot of it), have evolved mechanisms to strengthen themselves, with the plant version of a vertebrate's spine, probably in response to wind. They incorporate into their cellular structure minute quantities of silica as a stiffening agent. This means that grazing animals don't get a free lunch: eventually the tough prairie grasses grind down the teeth of those who eat them.

Despite this built-in toughness, the blue grama looks soft. Two young women stopped to admire the lawn and commented on how soft it looked. I invited them to kick off their sandals and try it. They did and giggled at the pleasing texture and caress on their bare feet.

Corralled by driveway and paved street, blue grama still manages to look wild – a little dishevelled and undomesticated. When it greens up in the spring, later than other lawns, it retains a subtle, pale shade – muted and not showy like the grab-your-eyes deep green of the misnamed Kentucky bluegrass. In the autumn, it wisely senesces and goes dormant early, leaving behind a tan mat of wool with occasional seed heads poking skyward.

I've given away our nonmotorized push mower. It made a pleasant clicking noise as the spiral blade cycled around, and it was good for a little exercise every week or so through the summer. But like tossing one's crutches aside at Lourdes, it felt freeing to let it go. The neighbours are probably curious as to how we are going to deal with the lawn. No one's asked, but if they do, I'll remind them that in the natural world, prairie grasslands were managed by either fire or grazing. It's their choice, I'll say – we can either torch the lawn periodically or get a buffalo in to graze it down.

A tiny patch of native blue grama grass doesn't seem like much of a statement against a backdrop of a highly artificial, much-manipulated city landscape. But I suppose the first footprint of European immigrants to the grasslands of southern Alberta wasn't initially very significant either. To recognize where we live, with the constraints of the landscape, is a faltering step to make. Ours is a tiny step of reversal but one we hope others try. Our prairie urban garden is a grassland home companion.

AGRICULTURE
A Love Story

———

Can the song of a meadowlark signal a shift in agriculture? I found that hopeful sign in one corner of Alberta, as well as a place where a love for the land and the craft of farming still survives.

Doom, gloom and despair seem to pervade other corners of agriculture, like rank and sturdy weeds. It's not a place where the word "love" is part of the conversation. Having grown up on a farm, I have empathy. My own mother, in a rare burst of profanity, once told me to "get the hell off the farm." Maybe she meant it in a different context, but the negative sentiment about agriculture is a common theme.

In this sea of negativity floats an island called Sunrise Farm, in east-central Alberta. There I was transported to a place of optimism, hope and solutions. It looked like a typical central Alberta farm at first blush, but then I noticed there was no array of expensive heavy metal lined up. No big, dual-wheeled four-wheel-drive tractor, no immense tillage equipment, no combine with a maw large enough to hoover up a small town, and, most telling, no sprayer.

Past a gate sign with a meadowlark frozen in song was a scene of green pastures, some with small groups of cattle managed with electric fences, and moveable pens housing poultry and pigs. These pens weren't cages, in the sense of industrial growth chambers for incarcerated animals, but rather outdoor spas where interaction with sun, grass and fresh air was the reality. I knew pigs couldn't fly, but watching them I hadn't realized they were capable of smiling. To engage in momentary anthropomorphism, they looked happy.

The chickens avidly hunted grasshoppers and settled into a new day of fresh greenery. They came from a commercial supplier, one who also provides to mega-sized, indoor poultry factories. Nothing in the background of these chickens had likely prepared them for this alien environment of the outdoors. It was as if these birds "were boldly going where none of their kind has gone before." This *Star Trek* reference proved to be a metaphor for the metamorphosis of Sunrise Farm with the earthly journey of Don and Marie Ruzicka on an unfamiliar pathway.

As so many farmer's sons have done, Don initially left the farm but returned to conventional agriculture – grain farming with large equipment and a reliance on artificial inputs to maintain crop production. It was a period of extreme stress brought on by mounting debt, little or no financial return, and the beginning of medical issues perhaps exacerbated by stress and agricultural chemicals. As Don related, "It wasn't fun and I knew this style of farming was a dead end for us."

He and Marie arrived at a holistic management course looking for a viable alternative to being locked into a financial funnel that typifies conventional agriculture. A farm is just a flow-through mechanism for cash, and little adheres to the farm or the farmer. What holistic management started them on was a systems approach, a pathway to understanding interactions, interconnections and interdependencies in their lives and with their land. It was the recognition that the pathway forward for the farm involved mimicking and respecting Nature, not bludgeoning her into submission.

As I interacted with Don, I sensed someone who is thoughtful, introspective and observant, with the additional ability to think critically. Don acknowledged that he went through his own version of *Silent Spring*, the ecological classic by Rachel Carson. "The meadowlarks had disappeared and the farm lacked their burst of song. As I plowed up native grass to expand my grain fields, the sharp-tailed grouse that had danced for centuries disappeared." That evidence of critical thinking would surface several times, or as Don joked, "You can observe a lot, just by watching."

His moveable poultry pens, filled with coyote food units, a.k.a. chickens and turkeys, seemed like a predator's buffet. I was a bit incredulous about the prospect of leaving all those plump poultry out overnight in the middle of a field without guard dogs, search lights and shotguns. I thought the morning would reveal nothing more than piles of feathers. Don reassured me my worries were groundless. Predation wasn't an issue, nor had he resorted to draconian protection techniques or lethal means of control. "I've watched coyotes," he said, "and noticed they are reluctant to make an attack when they are uncertain of the surroundings." That made sense. Over a century of being shot at, trapped, chased with dogs and poisoned would compel an exaggerated amount of alertness for survival. What intrigued me was Don's ability to use his observations of coyote behaviour to make his poultry operation tamper-proof.

Coloured plastic poultry crates were arranged around the pens, seemingly randomly. Some had articles of clothing on them. It didn't look like the Maginot Line of defence, but as each was changed every few days, it must have set up a sense of disquiet in a coyote's mind. Then there was the evening entertainment, not to soothe a turkey's troubled brain but to trick a coyote one. A radio was left playing overnight, and the combination of music and human voices proved an effective deterrent to coyote midnight munchies.

It's said music calms the savage beast – Don was unsure of this. He tuned the radio to either CBC or to a Christian rock station. At the end of one season, when the birds had all been processed, Don had inadvertently left the radio playing in the field. On his return, he noticed coyotes had chewed the wire from the battery, silencing the radio. Unfortunately, it was unclear which station the radio was tuned to, so one must draw one's own conclusions about coyote listening preferences.

On the surface, this seemed like an innovative way to escape predation on poultry. It was also an acknowledgement on Don's part that he needed coyotes. "If you're going to farm holistically you must realize the value of all the pieces. Coyotes are one of the pieces of our farm." They just don't get a share of the chickens, I realized.

Then there are the bees. Insects hover well beneath our radar of consciousness. "Yet, on average, every third bite of food is compliments of a pollinating insect, usually a bee," explained Mark Wonneck, an ecologist with Agriculture Canada. We are seldom aware of the protection and advantages afforded us by natural predators, insect pollinators and soil organisms. Rachel Carson called it a "walk unseeing through the world." We are blissfully unaware of the intricate system, with all the attendant complexity, that supports us. If you're going to farm with nature, paying attention to the little things is essential.

It's the little things, the unseen things, that together are vastly more important than we can imagine, like soil and the wee beasties that inhabit it. Dr. John Dormaar, Emeritus Soil Scientist for Agriculture Canada, said of soil it was "the excited skin of the earth," yet we treat it like dirt. With conventional agriculture, that life is literally blasted and burned with annual injections of anhydrous ammonia fertilizer, used to artificially inflate crop yields. In turning his back on that approach, Don acknowledged, "The little things those little things do add up to big things."

And so, on Sunrise Farm, 45,000 trees and shrubs later, wetlands restored, riparian areas managed for health, and all the cultivated acres reseeded to perennial pasture, there was the thrumming summer sound of biodiversity, especially of bees. It was a bit overwhelming with the additional orchestra of birds. If one's hearing was discriminating enough, an ear to the ground might have discerned a harmonious hum as well.

It takes farmers like the Ruzickas to understand that natural systems have inherent values – a long history of integration, cooperation, efficiency, resilience and regeneration. Natural systems are the archetype of the perfect assembly line. Working with them involves a paradigm shift from conventional agriculture, especially acknowledging the interrelationship of components and an organization that shouldn't be deconstructed. What Don did was to keep all the pieces and allow them to act in a unified, natural whole.

To maintain and tap into that marvellously well-adapted natural system is to understand sustainability at an elemental level. Keeping the system ticking doesn't involve significant financial resources, nor does it require the use of artificial, interventionist tactics. What it does require is a person like Don with observational skills, intuition, imagination, patience and humility. In his words, "We don't need to add anything to the land; we just have to quit subtracting from it."

None of the conventional approaches to agriculture seemed to the Ruzickas to be oriented to working within a natural system to create resilience or towards long-term care of the soil, the thin veneer upon which all of us survive. The economic, ecological and social implications were wide reaching and sobering. And nowhere in agribusiness was there any accounting for meadowlarks. Don characterized the effect of reversing their path as "getting two anvils off his shoulders." As Wendell Berry remarked, "When going back makes sense, you are going ahead."

That would be the small-scale organic, free range, grass-fed, permaculture, no growth hormones, no antibiotics, pesticide/ herbicide free, direct marketing, "you pick," artisan, community-based, low-input, "green" forms of agriculture whose focus is on food production and distribution at local and regional scales. In many ways these represent the antithesis of agribusiness.

It can be said crops now produced on most farms are thoroughly "watered" with fossil fuel. To put it into perspective, Don's farm operated on a few sips of fossil fuel. His weekly measure of fuel would be gulped in a few hours of conventional farming. An urban commuter probably burns more gas in a week than did Don. In reducing fuel and other costs, Sunrise Farm followed that ageless though seldom heeded truism of agriculture, "It's not so much what you make in farming; it's what you get to keep."

Sunrise Farm operated mainly with sunshine, biological activity, the recycling of plant and animal material, and Don's footsteps. It and these other "fringe" farms could be considered a return to where agriculture came from; there we might find sustainable forms of agriculture for the future.

Some would say it is abject sentimentality to talk of love when one discusses agriculture. Today, recasting agriculture as agribusiness creates an orthodoxy of an unsentimental, hard-nosed, economic "bottom line" endeavour. It is as if the process of growing things is viewed as a factory manufacturing widgets or grommets instead of food. But Sunrise Farm was a unique example, where one can turn to the word *love* to describe the relationship of its keepers, its caretakers, to the land.

Don and Marie learned that wealth existed in the natural glory around them and recalibrated their desires to be satisfied with a mountain bluebird rather than bushels of malt barley. The argument that it doesn't pay the bills or put food on the table is laughably false, especially as we tucked into barbequed pork and a bounty of garden vegetables, followed by fresh strawberries.

The Irish saying, "Enough is a feast" came to mind. Perhaps, as Bill McKibben, an environmental educator relates, "An awful lot of the rest of what we want is not necessary, and pursuing it means wrecking what we have." The meadowlark and the shopping mall are mutually exclusive.

Likely what occurred on Sunrise Farm isn't for everyone; maybe the proportion of farmers engaging in this new-old order will always be small. Proportions aside, this farm with the song of meadowlarks resonating represents a decision point for agriculture, one agriculture agencies and consumers would do well to heed. In a world of rapacious economic theory, where bigger is always deemed better, many of us have become increasingly suspicious of the mantra and direction. The Ruzickas had decided that Sunrise Farm would be small, not because it can't be big but because it can be better.

As I walked the rich pastures and the diverse woodlots, and paused beside the numerous wetlands of Sunrise Farm, it struck me the place was the antithesis of "agribusiness." I'm surrounded with a sense of peace and harmony with birds and bees and cows and water. It was a warm, comfortable, serene feeling, and the closest description possible for that sense of well-being is contentment. The farm showed the care of its stewards. It struck me that caring is the root of love.

Meadowlarks began to sing again, in 2000, just 11 years after their disappearance. I sensed Don and Marie saw in that return a vindication of all their considerable efforts to transform themselves. What changed to convince meadowlarks to return to Sunrise Farm? I think the most significant change was in Don and Marie – farmers who developed an ethic of care and love for their land.

In the words of Thich Nhat Nanh, a Buddhist monk, "People usually consider walking on water or in thin air a miracle. But I think the real miracle is not to walk on water or in thin air, but to walk on earth." Don and Marie walk the earth of Sunrise Farm thoughtfully, intelligently and lightly. They are an inspiration and, if others would emulate them, we could fix an ailing piece of Alberta's landscape – the rural, agricultural one. That would be a miracle, one within our grasp.

TRACKS AND SPOOR

Golden yellow aspen leaves quietly rustle in the Porcupine Hills. The noise of summer motors no longer overwhelms the breath of wind caressing the ancient Douglas firs. Emerson wrote, "Let us be silent, that we may hear the whispers of the gods." The motorized set has either not heard or not understood the message, drowned out as it is in the screaming of fossil-fuelled piston action. Perhaps the gods of off-highway vehicle (OHV) users have to shout to be heard.

Today, on a glorious autumn day, it is Emerson's gods, the ones with soft, subtle voices, who are speaking. They remind me that I am in a place named by the Blackfoot for the outline of trees on ridgetops, set against an improbably big sky at the edge of endless grassland. The Porcupine Hills must have appeared like a welcome antidote to the grasslands, where, at times, it seems there is nothing to lean your eyes on.

I have the labyrinth of trails to myself, unlike in the summer, and I find myself paying close attention to the stories engraved on this landscape. This thought pattern becomes a trap, and, instead of just looking and enjoying the subtle shifts of emphasis, I start to ponder what I observe. Colin Fletcher, the Welsh-born voice of hikers, wrote, "In beautiful places, thought can be an impediment to pleasure."

But it's too late for subtle appreciation as I try to make sense of the pair of women's panties beside the trail, and a few feet later a pair of men's underwear. Modesty prevents me from providing further description of these underpinnings, especially size, but I would characterize both as ample.

I'm not a competent enough tracker to read whether one set of underwear was meant as bait or a signal for the other. Perhaps it was a case of one merely reacting to the other, or a spontaneous gesture by both. I'm on a well-used OHV trail, and, as the OHV people like to point out, this is a family sport. I just didn't realize conception on trail-side was part of it, adding erection to the cycle of traction, compaction, erosion and sedimentation.

Maybe those of us who use our natural quads for back-country travel are missing something. Do the vibrations, pounding, bouncing, tension and torsion, plus the harmonic engine whine, induce a hypnotic state that excites passion and brings out naked, trailside lust? Is it mixed up in display, with mud-gripper tires shooting up a rooster tail of dirt and rocks to indicate fitness to breed? Part of the ritual must be the ability to explore new horizons by carving deep ruts into steep slopes.

Prospective mates must discern this activity as an indication of superior foraging ability. Maybe it's the rhythmic booming, farting exhaust – a primitive tribal drum call for an elaborate mating ceremony.

That's what I'm thinking while observing the spoor of the summer motorheads. But it is difficult to stalk the elusive OHV user to understand their rituals. Maybe these artifacts weren't part of a mating ritual – the dance with no pants – but instead an alternative headgear to filter dust from a busy trail. All the trails I walk on are layered in dust; it puffs up under my boots. At speed, with a pack of quads or trail bikes, the scenery must be completely blotted out.

The trails I walk are rutted, in some places ground down to bedrock. Spinning wheels have advanced the rate of geologic-al weathering and speeded up erosion far beyond the natural scale. I do some cross-sectional measurements of trail sections to see how far down motorized traffic has worn them.

My back-of-the-envelope calculations shock me. On nearly flat to moderate slopes, for every four paces, up to a half a ton of soil has eroded away. On steeper slopes, approximately a ton of soil has slipped downslope, again every four paces. Occasion-al mini Grand Canyons have formed on the very steep hillsides where water has finished the job begun by spinning tires. Down to bedrock and unnavigable even by OHVs, new trails now parallel these tank traps, hastening the eventual widening of the canyons.

One of the trails extends from the road in the valley bottom to the ridgetop, about 1.5 kilometres. For a trail that rarely ex-ceeds a metre in width, something approximating 300 tons of soil has eroded away. If this were farmland, the rate of erosion would galvanize action to stop it. And this is just one of myriad trails criss-crossing the Porcupine Hills.

Unknowingly, people driving on these trails have created a perfect storm of erosion in the Porcupine Hills. Every trail, every rut is a conduit, a straight-line feature that captures water from snowmelt and rainfall. These linear trails are an efficient interception and collection system, hastening the rush of water downslope. In their efficiency is the problem. To decrease erosion, a watershed needs water to move slowly, at a constrained pace hindered and thwarted by vegetation. That way the speed of moving water, an erosive force, is reduced and more of it seeps into the soil, creating a reservoir of water for drier periods. Like slow food, we need slow runoff.

Gravity is a formidable force, and the soil loosened by tires and aided by runoff waters finds its way downhill. Beneath me, in the valley bottom, is Beaver Creek. One doesn't have to connect many dots to imagine where all the soil eroding from the trails is headed.

But I suppose someone without enough sense to pick up their underwear from beside the trail probably hasn't grasped the simplest principles of hydrology (like "Water runs downhill") or of erosion ("Bare soil, like a bare bottom, moves"). Just because we have technology doesn't mean we also have wisdom.

Beaver Creek, once a stream that babbled along over gravel with water clear enough to see the bottom, now muddles through banks of mud, the result of former hill slopes brought low by incessant tire action. The creek, tiny at best, struggles with this undue load of sediment, equivalent to an incredibly long line of trucks with tandem loads of dirt toiling up to dump it all into the waters of Beaver Creek every year, year after year.

Researchers have found sediment runoff from OHV activity to be two to 20 times higher than the runoff rate from undisturbed ground, depending on slope, precipitation and intensity of vehicle use. Insidiously, cumulatively, this sediment pours off bare slopes and down rutted trails past the passersby, most of whom are oblivious to the phenomenon.

Imagine the reaction if you brought just one truckload of dirt up to Beaver Creek and dumped it into the water. You'd risk prosecution under a number of federal and provincial statutes. If someone from the Beaver Creek watershed group caught you, there might be some old-fashioned western justice meted out – the type that involves no courtrooms and no lawyers.

I don't actually think any of the ranchers of the Beaver Creek watershed group would engage in vigilante justice, but it must be frustrating, even infuriating, to have worked for nearly a decade on restoration and improved management of their lands only to look upstream and see the public land, the Forest Reserve, treated so poorly.

When the upstream owner is the Alberta government, wouldn't you think that a stewardship ethic would be present, and that there would be attempts to manage land uses to prevent excessive erosion?

The Porcupine Hills are dangerously close to turning into a piston-head racetrack and obstacle course with industrial overtones of petroleum development and clear-cut logging. It's happened over time, with the acquiescence of the land manager, the Alberta government. It's classic benign neglect. Before this landscape disappears completely in a pall of dust and is swallowed up by vehicle ruts, before the streams become paved with mud, some reflection and rethinking are necessary.

Like the couple responding to stimuli on trailside, leaving their underwear behind, OHV users have responded to a void in resource management in our forest reserves. This has proliferated beyond the capacity of the land to absorb such use. Aldo Leopold explained the issue of roads and trails (and OHVs) with the metaphor of the pig in the parlour. He elaborated, in 1925:

> Roads and wilderness are merely a case of the pig in the parlor. We now recognize that the pig is all right – for bacon, which we all eat. But there no doubt was a time, soon after the discovery that many pigs meant much bacon, when our ancestors assumed that because the pig was so useful an institution he should be welcomed at all times and places. And I suppose that the first 'enthusiast' who raised the question of limiting his distribution was construed to be uneconomic, visionary, and anti-pig.

Like Leopold's pigs, we can have too many trails and too many OHVs on them.

Caring for the Porcupine Hills should take us back to the basics. First, we need to protect the watershed, a priority higher than any other. We can accomplish this by first restoring, then maintaining a healthy landscape, one that is resilient to erosion, traps moisture and is composed of native plants. That goes a long way towards securing habitat for fish and wildlife. Caring means we have to reverse the syndrome of detachment and denial, where people who foul and despoil landscapes do not think of how their activity affects the natural world or anyone else.

As we secure the physical place, we also need to secure a place for it in our minds, maybe in our hearts. At the end of

A Sand County Almanac, Aldo Leopold writes: "Recreational development is a job not of building roads into lovely country, but of building receptivity into the still unlovely human mind."

We need an old-growth forest of the mind, a watershed of thought, an ecosystem of empathy and a landscape of understanding. In that place, there needs to be respect for and awareness of the natural world, as well as a sense of limits.

We can create that place, where peace and quiet provides an antidote to our otherwise busy, noisy lives. There, we might experience the natural world and all of its treasures, benefits and glories, as will future generations of enlightened citizens. We will hear the whispers of the gods, and our footprint will be fleeting and light.

WHO SPEAKS FOR ENDANGERED SPECIES?

There is a tendency on the part of some sectors (notably industry, some landowners and, remarkably, governments at all levels) to see protection of endangered species as a conspiracy to rob them of privileges and opportunities. It just isn't that simple.

If all of us would step back from the rhetoric and hand-wringing over entitlements, conspiracy theories, perceived economic loss, usurping of provincial rights by federal decree, perception of personal property rights infringement, and the mythical heavy hand of government, we might see another perspective.

Wild species are going missing at a rate unparalleled since dinosaurs disappeared. The root cause of this, especially with grassland species, is our practice of using up most of the space for our purposes. That human use has involved cultivation, urban development, petroleum extraction, transportation networks and myriad smaller endeavours, all of which have caused the cumulative game-changing shifts and shrinkage of native habitat to a shadow of what was formerly available.

The intent of species-at-risk legislation is to rebalance the stakes in favour of imperilled species, giving them a lifeboat of sorts so as to reduce the risk of them sinking out of existence.

Sage grouse are caught in the controversy between those who see diminished population status as a failure to manage and protect habitat and those who see efforts to stem the tide of possible extirpation as conflicting with free and full economic opportunity.

When we reach the edge of a cliff, as we have with sage grouse, the alternatives disappear. Either we do something to arrest the downward trend in grouse numbers, or we step back and watch them disappear from Alberta after a residency of approximately 12,000 years. Species-at-risk legislation fortunately won't allow us to take the latter easier route, no matter how comfortable and economically advantageous it might seem to be.

There is precious little wiggle room left, after years of government foot dragging in the race to exploit natural resources. The tired old refrains of mitigation, more research, and enhanced land-use guidelines are an attempt to drag the debate on longer without actually doing anything helpful for grouse recovery. Einstein's words, "We can't solve problems by using the same kind of thinking we used when we created them," resonates strongly.

We can't or don't bother to recall what the landscape looked like when the ecosystem was in balance. There is an expectation, based on no evidence, that sage grouse will persist on fragmented landscapes as we pile compromise upon compromise to "resolve" each new calamity.

It is an oft-repeated theme with many of Alberta's similarly imperilled wild species, including Westslope cutthroat trout, bull trout, caribou, and a long list of species not yet imperilled but queuing up for that designation. Pronghorn antelope, another iconic species of Alberta's prairie, also finds itself in an increasingly fragmented and diminished grassland world.

The sage grouse dilemma is a result of a classic failure to plan, the timidity of resource management, the inability to see and respond to critical thresholds, and the intransigence of all of us to act responsibly, quickly and decisively before a species fades into oblivion.

All of us – governments, industry, academia, conservationists, landowners and the public – have a duty to ensure that sage grouse (and others) are allowed to survive and recover. The debate isn't about whether they should be saved but rather how to save them and how quickly we need to act. Two essentials for any wild species are place and space. In the case of sage grouse, like all species, they and their habitats are intertwined and incapable of being separated.

If we took the perspective that we are building our province and our communities to last forever instead of just to the next election, or the next resource revenue check, or the next shopping trip, our take on endangered species would be remarkably different, I think. We need to face the hard question: Are we stewards of the land and all of its resources or are we trapped in a spiral of instant gratification and gluttony with no sense of responsibility to future generations?

If we can protect some places and spaces for sage grouse and allow the recovery of populations to more robust levels, the intended effects will benefit other species. It may well be that our own species will need these places with healthy biodiversity and abundant ecosystem services.

It shouldn't be just the Canadian government speaking for endangered species; it should be all of us. As fellow travellers on a finite planet, it is our obligation to keep, as the ecologist Aldo Leopold admonished us, "every cog and wheel."

In *The Lorax*, Dr. Seuss also provides some essential advice that we might apply to endangered species: "Unless someone like you cares a whole awful lot, nothing's going to get better. It's not."

Who speaks for endangered species? We all should!

MITIGATION
Cosmetics or Compensation?

———

My neighbour Steve once had a tall, majestic cottonwood tree in his backyard. In urban environments, trees have obvious value. They provide wind and sun protection, both of which are crucial in southern Alberta. Birds are attracted to them for nesting, foraging and cover. People are drawn to trees too. Because of the higher humidity under the canopy, it feels cooler there on a blistering hot August afternoon. Property values increase because of the amenity value of mature trees.

I can only guess that one of the branches of that cottonwood tapped on Steve's bedroom window during windy periods. My neighbour, now gone to his reward, wasn't a destructive or uncaring soul, but in this instance, he had a blind spot. The "solution" started innocently enough with Steve wielding his chainsaw to trim off the offending branch. Things went south very quickly thereafter.

In a quirk I have seen in myself and other men, once started there is no such thing as a *little* trimming. When wielding that saw, Steve's eyes must have glazed over and thoughts of consequences became temporarily suspended. In that regard, his response can be characterized as little different than the institutional blindness brought on by development's imperative: "Ready, fire, aim!"

Steve fired up his chainsaw to cut off the one offending limb but became so taken with the effort he didn't quit until the tree was a bare three-metre-high stump. This too has remarkable resonance with the larger world. We emerge from the trance-like state of largely unplanned development and then begin to ask how we might compensate for its effects.

In my neighbour's case, what appeared on top of the stump was a brightly painted birdhouse. I suppose it may have been an act of contrition to mitigate his act of arboricide. The cotton-wood trunk leafed out for a couple of years, but those few leaves could not sustain the tree. It is now dead. It cannot offer shade or shelter ever again. Neither will it capture and store energy, filter the air or provide a pleasing aspect to the landscape.

The gaily painted birdhouse mitigates the loss of none of these values and was the final act of putting lipstick on a corpse. Sadder yet, no bird has made use of this artificial habitat for years.

Looking out from my backyard into Steve's has provided me a tangible and enduring sense of what mitigation often means. A failure to recognize the worth of an intact system. An inability to correctly assess the advantages and virtues, so that any attempts at compensation, to "mitigate" the damage, are inadequate. Add to that no effective monitoring to test the efficacy of mitigation: Did it work? Steve's birdhouse has become a metaphor for mitigation.

If the world isn't going to be perfect, don't you just yearn for one that is at least a bit more honest? Even though it wouldn't diminish the issue, imagine if business, industry and governments were a little less disingenuous about the impacts of their activities.

"Look, this drilling project will trash the native prairie grassland," they could say. "Caribou are toast, as are grizzlies, sage grouse and bull trout." Or, "This new dam will dry the river up, but we'll produce more potatoes and power for more microwaves." Or, "We cannot, in this lifetime, or perhaps in several lifetimes, reclaim this massive hole where a mountain used to exist in the Eastern Slopes."

These are unlikely statements in today's world. What we are more likely to hear is, "No wildlife will be harmed and every blade of grass will be replaced." Empty words masquerading under the term "mitigation," full of promise but low on substance.

In a development-focused ideology with no land-use strategy, "No" is rarely an acceptable answer in the face of potential development. Mitigation might be thought about in the same way that technological solutions are employed in smoking, ostensibly to reduce the health risk but really to maintain consumption rates. The use of filtered cigarettes precisely fits this thinking. The tobacco industry tries to solve a problem in a way that lets consumption of the drug continue without interruption.

Mitigation addiction is based on the vain hope that we can continue to do everything, everywhere, anytime, and all the time, with our development footprint effectively erased behind us.

Mitigation has become one of those aggrandizing bureaucratic terms that assigns a human intent to compensate for a loss, without a clear statement about how the bargain will be struck. Mitigation is politically sound but ecologically risky. It may be the most potent public relations rhetoric yet to rationalize the loss of a river, a forest or a piece of prairie.

When I say "mitigate," you probably think of concepts like "fully compensate, replace, restore, reclaim, restitution, fair, equitable." But what I meant is "trade-off, substitute, appropriate balance, offset, alleviate, mollify, lighten." You may leave thinking you understand, with an assurance of a positive outcome; you will invariably end up unhappy and dissatisfied. Mitigation is a long, smooth-sounding word that conceals its dangers, as long, smooth words do. The danger is there, nevertheless, as is the potential for misunderstanding and manipulation.

We should reject outright the tendency to believe that mitigation provides fair and equitable compensation for losses and that mitigation is always successful. Some mitigation techniques work some of the time, in some locations, and with some species. Unlike a categorical "No" to development, there is no mitigation silver bullet that has a universal application.

A long list of reviewers have found that the mitigation castle is built on the shifting sands of inadequate baselines, a failure to measure, a lack of standardized measurements, little transparency in reporting, inappropriate timelines and inadequate resources. An inability to understand complex interrelationships and the inevitable oversimplification results in mitigation plans missing the mark. Enthusiasm, resources and monitoring never last long enough to see the task to completion. We stop long before the end with the rationalization that something is better than nothing.

Mitigation as a strategy to deal with relentless development pressures isn't going to disappear, nor should it. At best, mitigation sensitizes us to the very real losses and trade-offs that are an inherent part of development on any landscape. Effective mitigation employs adaptive management: learning and applying new knowledge along the way. Unfortunately, the only way to learn is to constantly evaluate the actions taken. Stronger measures are needed to ensure that monitoring (and reporting) occurs and that resources are budgeted for the lifespan of the initiative.

Mitigation without evaluation is like a contract without a signature, essentially a worthless gesture. What we don't talk about is the strategy for failure – what to do if the mitigation doesn't work. If there is no cost to failure, one might expect it to occur frequently.

When Aldo Leopold's bird dog Gus couldn't find pheasants, he worked up an enthusiasm for meadowlarks. To quote Leopold, "This whipped-up zeal for unsatisfactory substitutes masked his failure to find the real thing. It assuaged his inner frustration." To assuage our inner frustration over the lack of a stewardship ethic, we have found us a meadowlark called "mitigation." Like the meadowlark, it has its good points. It smells like success but is often used to divert our attention from something more fundamental. Our real task is to learn to live within the limits of the land, and as Leopold exhorted, "To live on a piece of land without spoiling it."

RIPARIAN RECOVERY, NATURALLY

———

By the early 1970s the North Raven River (then known as Stauffer Creek) was no longer a happy creek. It was well on its way from being a shaded, meandering trout heaven to being cow-blasted, cultivated, and "civilized" with channelization.

The headwaters spring had become a hog wallow. Cattle had broken down stream banks, and the willow bottomlands had been cleared for grazing and cultivation. One farmer had straightened his portion of the creek, believing the meander bends took up too much valuable pasture. Sediment from crop fields poured into the stream after every rain, covering trout spawning gravels. The synergistic series of events combined to replace a narrow, deep, meandering stream with one that was wide, shallow and warm. This allowed pike and suckers to move upstream, into what had been classic trout waters.

Almost 50 years ago, Mel Kraft (Alberta Fish and Wildlife) and Elmer Kure (Alberta Fish and Game Association) started to discuss with central Alberta farmers along the North Raven River the possibility of restoring the sport fishery of this spring-fed stream. Their intent was to mitigate the effects of decades of unmanaged livestock use and cultivation on a stream that had developed a stellar reputation as a trout fishery.

The trend seemed clear, and it was downhill for the trout. Painfully, the inventory information was collected to confirm the trajectory, determine the solutions and pinpoint where restoration was required. Several reaches of the stream were electrofished to determine trout numbers and to set a biological benchmark against which recovery could be assessed. This common survey technique uses electricity to attract fish for capture. After measurement the fish are released and suffer no ill effects.

One reach of the creek had been cleared for pasture, and few willows remained. At one meander bend, a dead willow provided scant cover over a deep pool. There, we repeatedly caught a lone brown trout, weighing almost four kilograms. There was precious little habitat left in the stream for a fish of that size. That one trout, in one of the last pieces of survival habitat, was emblematic of the state of the stream and the urgency of recovery efforts.

A program of land acquisition, trades and agreements secured some tenure. Streambank fencing, limited stream crossings, and off-stream water developments were negotiated and constructed to give some of the vital and remaining bits of the riparian area some relief from agricultural pressures.

The recovery has been astonishing. It's as though the stream was just waiting for someone to take the pressure off and let the vegetation rebound and the banks rebuild. The willow growth is now thick enough that some anglers complain about the impenetrable tangle. In compensation, anglers are treated to a summer symphony of song from yellow warblers, house wrens, western wood-pewees, catbirds and yellowthroats. Sometimes, when anglers are thrashing through the willow jungle to access the stream, they hear a crash ahead as a moose escapes from a leafy refuge.

As the stream narrowed and deepened, the sediment was flushed out, and the increasingly abundant overhanging cover provided cooler temperatures, the trout population responded. Over a 20-year period, trout numbers increased more than

500 per cent; in areas that remained unmanaged, populations dropped by 80 per cent over the same time period.

In my mind, one of the outstanding aspects of the recovery of the North Raven River was the lack of an engineered human fingerprint, other than fences, on the stream. Success was achieved by working with the natural system – letting the stream re-naturalize and dictate the terms of mitigation. If one did not know the restoration history, it would be easy to conclude that the stream always looked as it does now.

The job in the area isn't done yet. Portions of the watershed still require changes, and even the functioning bits need tune-ups. However, the riparian and trout recovery on the North Raven River represents a model of mitigation effectiveness, one that needs to penetrate and guide mitigation thinking.

THE OLDMAN DAM
Beautiful Strategies, Ugly Facts

———

I heard the announcement approving the construction of the Oldman Dam on the truck radio as I was driving past the place where dam construction would shortly begin. This was not unfamiliar territory, as I had measured trout habitat, identified aquatic insects and caught trout in all of the three valleys to be flooded, before there was a whisper of any plans for dam construction. As I thought of the flooding of these majestic valleys, with some of Alberta's best fly-fishing opportunities, my heart sank.

The Oldman Dam, in southwestern Alberta, arguably has had the highest profile for mitigation in the province and the most scrutiny of mitigation effectiveness of any provincial initiative. Stung with quips like "only the Alberta government would destroy three rivers with one dam" (an act of uncharacteristic economy), the government had a considerable appetite for mitigation to counter substantial opposition to the prospect of inundating three Blue Ribbon trout rivers.

The project itself was mitigation on two separate fronts. Announced in the epicentre of a drought, it proposed additional water storage to compensate for the historically overallocated and overused St. Mary, Belly and Waterton rivers and to alleviate the difficulty Alberta had in meeting its interprovincial water-sharing agreement at the Saskatchewan border.

Faced with the inundation of 43.2 kilometres of the Castle, Crowsnest and Oldman rivers and their riparian forests, the task of putting a positive face on the project was daunting. Beyond the posturing, politicking and wordsmithing, the basics of the mitigation program revolved around replacing the loss of about 225,000 square metres of high-quality trout habitat and compensating for the loss of riparian forests with the protection, enhancement or creation of 689 wildlife habitat units. The promise was that this would restore fish and wildlife populations to pre-dam levels. Beautiful strategies they were, full of hope and promise. What followed, though, were ugly facts.

The first bit of ugliness, on the fisheries front, was where to find a place to plunk 225,000 square metres of new fish habitat. Of the three rivers affected, the Crowsnest River had the greatest history of channelization, urban development, transportation corridors and industrial development, especially related to coal mining and processing. It was a river with lots of old wounds that habitat mitigation could only partially correct. It was also an inherently productive river for trout. Very few opportunities for habitat mitigation presented themselves on the Castle and Oldman rivers. A little more than 100,000 square metres of high-quality habitat was shoehorned into the Crowsnest River, from just upstream of Coleman and downstream to the full supply level of the reservoir.

What was designed, and attempts made to construct, was deep-water habitat, the lack of which was felt to be a key limiting factor for trout. Trout require deep water for resting areas, to periodically escape higher-velocity portions of rivers. During winter conditions, as flows are reduced and ice cover thickens, the deep pools provide overwinter survival habitat.

This river re-creation required substantial river "training" with large boulder structures, which narrowed the channel and increased water velocity to scour deep pools. An ugly fact was that rivers don't respond well to training, especially over time. Imagine a solid, static object in a dynamic, moveable channel and the challenge of integrating the two.

Bedload movement (the downstream shifting of gravels, sand and silt), coupled with the inexorable energy of moving water, meant that some structures worked and others failed. With the ceaseless pounding of water, plus two major flood events within six years, the amount of constructed habitat was reduced by two-thirds. What did survive didn't meet the test of best-quality, deep-water habitat.

While inventorying high-quality habitat and auditing its decrease were not easy tasks, they paled in comparison with the complexity of evaluating whether any of the work did fish any good. A tremendous amount of work, spread out over 15 years, was done in an attempt to document trout responses. If lack of deep-water habitat was a key limiting factor to trout, creating more should have resulted in more fish.

That wasn't the case, at least not in direct proportion to habitat creation. Habitat improvements allowed trout populations to spread out over longer reaches of river and, to some extent, allowed some trout to grow larger. But the expected result – many more trout – didn't happen. It would seem the natural carrying capacity of a river reach can only be improved to a certain degree with habitat enhancement, and then other limiting factors come into play.

As a substantial part of the wildlife mitigation program for the Oldman Dam, shelterbelt plantings were used in an attempt to compensate for significant riparian losses from reservoir construction. Despite heroic and expensive efforts to select appropriate species, reduce competition with weeds, and water trees for up to three years, the results proved dismal, and the riparian forests inundated by the Oldman Dam have not been functionally replaced. An unintended, unplanned benefit of perimeter fencing and livestock exclusion has been the natural regeneration and spread of native shrubs. This represents an incremental gain for wildlife habitat but comes nowhere near balancing the loss.

So let's review where we now stand on this mitigation initiative. We got a reservoir that has very little utility for trout because it's deep and unproductive, resembling a bathtub being constantly filled and emptied. We got a dab of upstream habitat creation, much of which repaired old ravages and to which trout didn't respond in kind. There has been no ongoing commitment to fund the maintenance of constructed habitats as the river continues to wear them away and bury them.

Charitably, then, after accounting for all the losses of constructed habitat, there is still a deficit of about 200,000 square metres of high-quality trout habitat if the commitment of the Oldman Dam mitigation strategy is to be met. After these initial mitigation attempts, most of the focus for compensation of lost trout habitat shifted downstream of the reservoir, where no biological baseline existed from which to calculate trout habitat mitigation. As it turned out, enthusiasm and budgets waned and very little downstream trout habitat was constructed. Without any help, and in some ways a surprise, a tailwater fishery for rainbow trout developed downstream of the reservoir. However, the huge deficit in lost trout habitat remains.

On the wildlife front, no replacement of the cottonwood gallery forests occurred. Most of the planted trees and shrubs died or are too scattered to provide replacement habitat for wildlife. Prairie falcons got some new nesting ledges on cliffs, and some marginal wetland habitat was replaced.

Mitigation of the impacts of reservoir construction on three southern Alberta rivers remains an example of initial commitment, planning, effort, funding and evaluation. But, as Winston Churchill intoned, "However beautiful the strategy, you should occasionally look at the results." Despite the enthusiasm and promises, in the final analysis there simply wasn't enough room or ability to mitigate the negative effects of reservoir construction on fish and wildlife habitat, and the losses remain unresolved.

This should serve to remind us of the often empty promise of mitigation to compensate for losses of habitat and fish and

wildlife populations. Mitigation promises can suck you into unrealistic expectations that losses can be made right. They can't,
and you end up feeling cheated. The result of mitigation efforts
is usually more one of cosmetics than of compensation.

4

Our Cousins, the Fish

Do not tell fish stories where the people know you; but particularly don't tell them where they know the fish.

— Mark Twain

NATIVE TROUT
Time Tested

—————

If one were to scroll back through the tenure of native trout and their ancestors, on a whiplash-inducing rush through deep time, one might begin to appreciate the varieties of geologic episodes that formed, rejumbled, buried and exhumed the landscapes of trout.

What native trout endured, evolved with and adapted to includes: encroaching seas; retreating seas; volcanic events; continental drift; crustal deformations; drainage captures; drainage separations; orogenies; folding; faulting; igneous bulges; uplifts; downcuts; multiple glacial events; millions of years of weathering and erosion; and extremes of fire, flood, ice and drought. The odds of a fish surviving that smorgasbord of natural events seems improbable. But trout did survive, and we should stand in awe of that finny exuberance.

Yet, in the last century, a mere blip in geologic time, the effects of the wheel, chainsaws, mines, dams, climate change and, to a degree, the fish hook have made the previous thousands of years of trout existence in Alberta seem benign.

Bull trout, Westslope cutthroat trout, Athabasca rainbows, mountain whitefish and Arctic grayling are native to our Eastern Slopes. Many generations ago, they came from other geographies and settled in those streams along the eastern side of the Continental Divide and onto the western fringes of the grasslands, parkland and boreal forest. From visitors and tourists, they became residents with a long, earned tenure. These species are ancient, but their future is precarious.

They are creatures limited to certain conditions, found in the watersheds in which they evolved for the past 12,000 years. There is no place to go back to – it doesn't exist anymore. They make their last stand here, in an ecology dramatically altered by us. Some populations, in watersheds both large and small, have been extirpated, a loss of unique genetic inheritance. All remaining populations hang on by a fin. Once these trout would have been counted in the thousands. Then it was hundreds, then dozens, then a dozen, and, for some, finally none. They are not headed to the final roundup – they are in it.

The combination of climate change, lack of connectivity, competition from non-native trout, and habitat loss is particularly devastating for native trout since it attacks them from different but cumulative angles. It's hard to find a good survival strategy that works simultaneously against multiple threats.

Nothing in their past experience provides any sort of adaptive solutions to changes that happened in an apparent split second of their lengthy existence. We seem unwilling to acknowledge the new normal in their disrupted world, and the chances of native trout adjusting to that altered state are slim.

Of the many alterations, one is the imposition of non-native trout species on existing native ones. Non-native trout hitched a free ride to the new universe, but it took native trout thousands upon thousands of years to sort things out in their new geography. We might start culling some of the weeds that are non-native trout, which have replaced and continue to compete with the rightful owners of the Eastern Slope watersheds. It is an unfolding drama of human meddling, with severe consequences.

As we further change the world of native trout, we forget to mourn a reduced and diminishing stock. So far, none of the native species in the hierarchy of official protection – not caribou, not white-bark pine, not bull trout, not cutthroat trout, not Athabasca rainbow trout, not Arctic grayling, not grizzly bears – have inspired managers to bring order to a large and increasing land-use footprint. Land-use plans may help, if they reduce our footprint and restore vital habitats. If we think we have improved the situation with a plan but with no will to implement it, we will eventually discover that we have fooled ourselves completely.

We are not protecting native trout from extinction: they are protecting us from an extinction of experience as we engage with and begin to understand a world beyond ourselves.

Native trout have been successfully tested by time, but will they stand the test of our time? Native trout can fade from our collective memory, just as their vivid colours dissipate once a trout is removed from the water. It will take some Herculean efforts to repaint watersheds with native trout. But if we don't try, we will leave behind an incomplete piece of art.

WHY CARE ABOUT A CUTTHROAT?

———

Have you ever touched a cutthroat trout? If you have, you're lucky, since very few of this native species still remain in Alberta. They are cool to the touch – wet and slippery. What you touch isn't just a fish. It's a living, wriggling history book, the embodiment of a landscape and a study in adaptability and resilience.

Cutthroat trout saw the last of the continental glaciers, those kilometre-thick blocks of ice that shaped most of Alberta, and still live beneath the rapidly receding alpine ice flows. These fish, early visitors to what would become Alberta, saw a raw land transformed and adapted to the changes. When they perceived the loss of bison, they may not have sensed that they were seeing a glimpse of their own future. As many of us settled the banks of rivers and lakes teeming with these hordes of fish, we probably thought they would last forever.

We could call the cutthroat one of the early pioneers, a species superbly adapted to its adopted world. What cutthroat have done is rolled the storms, the floods, the droughts, the changes in water temperature, the good and the bad – the natural variability of their world – into their genetic material as a mechanism for survival.

What they have not adapted to, cannot adapt to, is the speed and magnitude of changes we brought to their world in a period of time as short as a human life. Only a handful of mostly isolated populations survive in the province today. Contrast that image with the reality not so long ago, when cutthroats swam from the headwaters of the Oldman and Bow rivers as far downstream as the cities of Lethbridge and Calgary.

Cutthroat trout evolved to fit a particular environmental context, a place in the watersheds of the Oldman and Bow rivers. Their beauty is derived from that fitness. To see the flash of a cutthroat in a crystal-clear stream, a splash of liquid sunshine, is to experience a natural piece of art. That scene, with all of the intricacy and mystery of an interconnected system, is as valuable as a Renoir or Picasso and as irreplaceable.

Cutthroat trout are part of a watershed and an indicator of landscape health. The clarity of the medium in which cutthroat swim should jog our sensibilities and remind us of the source of our drinking water. Having cutthroat occupy these watersheds is the gold seal of water quality. The ripples that extend outward from a pebble dropped in a stream containing cutthroat inevitably find us.

But it's just a fish. Why should we care about cutthroat trout?

Nostalgia is not the driving force behind the desire to preserve populations of cutthroat trout. Rather, that aspiration derives from an acknowledgement of a species with a best fit for life in some of Alberta's waters, tested as cutthroat have been in the crucible of their habitats for at least 12,000 years. This fish has been entrusted to our care, not for our exclusive use and disposal but to ensure that viable populations are passed on, unimpaired, for subsequent generations. It would be a blot on our record as stewards of shared resources to allow a species like cutthroat trout to disappear through apathy, ignorance, inaction or greed.

There are also elements of practicality, sensibility, compassion and foresight in the push to protect cutthroat, to ensure they don't slip through our fingers and out of our consciousness. We would no more discard our history books, unravel the threads on a prized tapestry or weaken a bridge than we would allow an indicator of iconic landscapes, a connection with nature, or an essential ecosystem service to disappear.

If we can protect some places for the cutthroat and allow recovery of populations to more robust levels, the intended effects will benefit other species. It may well be that our own species will need these healthy watersheds with natural expressions of biodiversity. We truly need them now!

BULL TROUT
Watershed Sentinels

———

Bull trout arrived here in Alberta the hard way, the Darwinian way, across millions of years of randomness followed by some serendipity of passage near the tail end of glaciation. The journey exemplifies the point that adaptation isn't a sprint; it's a marathon.

Bull trout aren't glamorous, lacking the svelte lines and colours of the other native trout, like the cutthroat with its elegant orange jaw slash and splashes of colour. Bull trout are more like guided missiles – gray, utilitarian and lethal. They resemble baseball bats with fins and gills. Of course, who are we to critique the form by which evolution has met a functional demand? Bull trout, or at least their prototype, were swimming, fully formed, millions of years before we humans gained an upright stance.

Looks aside, that journey should give these fish equal standing with, if not priority over, economic interests related to dimensional lumber, nonrenewable energy sources or motorized recreation. In standard accounting practice, resource assets are put in the ledger column called "now," and that puts at risk the tomorrow for bull trout. Our rush to use and extract the wealth of the headwaters, in the now, has left an impoverished legacy.

If Albertans were to develop some personal connections and feelings for our provincial fish, somewhere between the pragmatism of following the law for species at risk and affection for a cherished fellow traveller, maybe the future would be less uncertain. As with aquatic creatures everywhere, until the presence of bull trout is finally detected by more than biologists, it is difficult to achieve recognition for their presence and create priority for their protection.

Bull trout are a unique, prehistoric population, a zoological rarity in many watersheds. We cannot let go of them by rationalizing that they are mere glacial relics and possibly doomed to elimination with our land-use practices, and with increasing emissions only accelerating that inevitability through higher water temperatures.

It is one thing to have a mystery surrounding the demise of a species throughout its historic range. It is quite another to know why and to have done so little to reverse the decline. Bull trout populations historically, and even in living memory, were abundant, but the current trend is grim. Pulling the lever to stop catch-and-keep angling has not restored population viability at a provincial scale. The species needs more than this policy of benign neglect leading to passive euthanasia.

If we are to continue to angle for them, the whole context of expectations and rewards must change. Bull trout cannot ever be considered again as just cheap protein. If we are to catch bull trout, it must be to visit them – to hold a cylinder of pure muscle and marvel at a creature that exists in a medium almost 800 times as dense as what us breathers of air experience. The next step will be to free the fish and then watch as it slips away into the depths and mysteries of water.

Many of us will want to fish for them, not only to connect but to reassure ourselves that bull trout and all they represent still exist. It might help us, in our hubris as humans, to occasionally be in the presence of a creature that epitomizes struggle and success. We can hold in our hand, however briefly, the test and the outcome of millennia of adaptation and evolution. We should be humbled by the experience. Should bull trout wink out of existence, what we are in danger of losing is an association with an ancient animal.

Within human memory, we have transformed our headwaters, the epicentre of bull trout populations, from a background of cold, clean, complex and connected habitats to ones markedly warmer, dirtier, simpler and fragmented. The condition of bull trout has been diagnosed, and the outcome need not be terminal, if we choose to act decisively, firmly and quickly.

It may be a startling new discovery that bull trout are inextricably linked to the landscape and stand (or swim) as an ecological surrogate, marker or symbol. We need to convey the message that this part, the bull trout, is emblematic of the whole – of watershed integrity and health. Our perception of bull trout might shift if we recognize them as the pinnacle of an ecosystem.

So do we have an obligation to protect bull trout? Native trout, bull trout included, are integrators and indicators, helping us understand our land-use footprint and the implications and consequences for essential things delivered from our watersheds, like reliable, high-quality water. Therein lies the reciprocal arrangement; bull trout are our sentinels. The presence and abundance of native trout signal a high degree of watershed health. Declines in these populations are a distant early warning signal about the intensity, frequency, type and cumulative impact of our land use.

That confers upon us an obligation to protect bull trout and the essential habitat upon which they rely. Inevitably, it isn't only about saving bull trout but also about saving ourselves. It is an endless fragile chain of interdependence, tenaciously intertangled, as is the life cycle of the bull trout within a watershed.

What is at stake with bull trout is the ecological stability and integrity of our headwaters. These are the places where protection should resonate, in our heads, our hearts and in our mouths, where our thirst is quenched. That thirst is physical, for those headwaters provide drinking water for two out of every three Albertans. It is also metaphoric because our headwaters are the remaining symbols of wildness, a heritage that each Albertan should carve a place for in our collective psyche.

A recovery strategy and recovery actions are required for bull trout because we don't want to write a eulogy for the species. Rather, we need to engage in writing a new chapter on securing a better future for this sentinel of our headwaters. Bull trout represent a species that was made to last. In letting them be what they are, we ensure our own future.

ARCTIC GRAYLING
Going, Going, Gone

———

The Arctic grayling is a dramatic fish, shiny with distinct scales and a large fin on its back that is sometimes as tall as its body is thick. They shimmer, even in tea-coloured water. With their huge dorsal fin, they seem more to sail through the water than to swim.

A member of the trout family, grayling swim in the waters of the boreal forest of Alberta and in the northern foothills. Their historic range was the entire Peace, Hay and Athabasca river basins.

Fisheries biologists point to a 40 per cent contraction in the range of grayling waters, most of which has happened in living memory. More than half of current grayling populations have been reduced to 10 per cent or less of historic population numbers.

Prior to the 1980s, the Beaverlodge and Redwillow rivers of northwestern Alberta were reported to support one of the largest spawning runs of Arctic grayling in Alberta. No grayling have been seen in the Beaverlodge River since 1994, and the species is now considered extirpated from that watershed. Populations in the Redwillow River are noted as "declining."

These astounding statements of fact are detailed in a massive investigative report entitled *Redwillow Watershed: An Overview of the History and Present Status of Fish Populations and Fish Habitat and Recommendations for Restoration.* The work was commissioned by the Alberta Fish and Wildlife Division for the watersheds of the Beaverlodge and Redwillow rivers and was completed in 2009.

Why did historically abundant populations of Arctic grayling, northern pike, bull trout and mountain whitefish disappear from the Beaverlodge River?

The finger of blame for population declines is usually pointed at fishing. From the 1920s to the early 1960s, it was legal to use traps strung across the channel to harvest fish on the Beaverlodge River for subsistence use. Arctic grayling (and presumably the other fish species) were canned for later use to eke out an existence in the far-off Peace region. But even this extreme use, combined with liberal sport fishing bag limits on grayling, was not the sole or even the most important cause of the collapse of these fish populations.

The authors of the report describe a perfect storm of cumulative, synergistic causes that resulted in crashes in fish numbers and distribution leading to the eventual extirpation of the Arctic grayling population. This is an insightful, cautionary tale of landscape-scale changes over less than a century, coupled with customary human blindness to the rate, impact and consequences of a series of seemingly unconnected land-use decisions.

Settlement in the Peace region began in the early 1900s, but it wasn't until the advent of powerful bulldozers in the early 1950s that significant changes began to appear in the watershed of the Beaverlodge River. Forest was rapidly replaced by agricultural fields; riparian fringes were narrowed and often disappeared. Wetlands were drained, and now roads interrupt drainage and channel flow, sending water to rivers faster and exacerbating floods.

The Beaverlodge River isn't fed by glaciers or snowmelt from mountains. The headwaters rise in the forested foothills, the rain barrel for catching, holding and slowly releasing water. As forest canopy was replaced by farm fields, the flood peaks rose higher with the faster release of snowmelt and rainfall to the river. Compared to memories of consistent flows throughout. the year, now the Beaverlodge River experiences greater floods in the spring and subsides to very low flows in the summer, often shrinking into a series of isolated pools by autumn.

The new normal for the flow regime is further complicated by short-sighted shoreline use. Changes in water quality also accompany a landscape transformed from forest to farms. Livestock have unrestricted access to stream banks, winter feeding on or near the water is common, and feedlots have been situated in close proximity to water. That combination, plus domestic sewage disposal and runoff from cultivated fields, brings not only sediment but a toxic agrochemical stew of fertilizers, herbicides and pesticides.

Up to the 1960s, residents of the watershed talked of good-quality water that was fit to drink and swim in, and that meant that the water was good for fish too. No one would voluntarily drink directly from or swim in the river now. The Beaverlodge River now has an excess of nutrients. A small amount of nutrients promotes growth and is beneficial in producing more of the things fish like to eat. Too much overwhelms the system – oxygen is robbed from the water and fish suffocate.

Arctic grayling are creatures of cool waters. Changing the way water is delivered, reducing flows in warmer periods of the year, and removing the shading effects of riparian vegetation allows river flow to heat up beyond the tolerance levels of fish.

Fish under stress – whether from temperature, low flows, impediments to movement or habitat loss – become more prone to infections and disease. Most of the sites sampled by Fish and Wildlife staff on the Beaverlodge River have revealed fish with deformities, disease, eroded fins, lesions and tumours – evidence of the toxic soup that flows down the river.

Arctic grayling hung on tenuously in the Beaverlodge River until sometime in the 1980s, and then they were gone.

It is perplexing that this happened in modern times, with some level of environmental consciousness and overlapping government responsibility. It speaks to institutional barriers that preclude action, poor communication between silos in government, and lack of oversight mechanisms coupled with a reluctance to regulate and enforce. Mostly, it speaks to our failure to plan for tomorrow, using existing evidence that would guide us onto a path of better decisions.

If the changes in the Beaverlodge River and the loss of fish provide a lesson, it is that fisheries management – maintaining fish – often has little to do with managing fish in terms of seasons, bag limits and harvest size. What dictates fish persistence or not is the integrity of the watershed and the elements that produce fish habitat. The additive effects of land and water use in the Beaverlodge River eroded the ability of fish to persist and eventually several species disappeared.

The phenomenon of Arctic grayling disappearance and the failure to react to this in any meaningful way plays out throughout the range of this native fish. In northeastern Alberta, in watersheds affected by tar sands development, the phrases most

commonly used to describe rivers and their grayling populations are "used to support," "had abundant populations" and
"historically contained." Harder to find are reports using the
terms "contains Arctic grayling." Nonexistent are ones where
Arctic grayling are described as "abundant," "large in size" and
"distributed widely." Sometimes the former presence of grayling has been discounted by industry as a fisherman's tale not
to be believed.

It was reported that, prior to the road being built to Fort
McMurray, you could catch hundreds of grayling in the House
River. Now there are none. In the Christina River, Martin Paetz,
the first fisheries biologist hired in Alberta and the head of the
Fisheries Branch for decades, reported catching 33 grayling
from one spot in less than an hour, in 1967. Twenty years later,
Martin returned, and he and a companion, fishing hard for two
days, caught seven grayling. Subsequently, over 200 fisheries
studies undertaken on the Christina between 2001 and 2010
managed, in that decade, to capture only two grayling.

In many watersheds, Arctic grayling are but a distant memory,
and even worse, if that could be imagined, have been forgotten
entirely. It is likely that the knowledge of missing Arctic grayling
populations has registered less in the public consciousness than
the knowledge that water occurs in the Martian atmosphere.

BULL TROUT GHOSTS

In a deep pool, beneath an immense logjam, I saw my first bull
trout. I didn't know then it was a bull trout; I was to learn that
much later. Precariously perched on that logjam, peering into

the deep water, that baseball bat–shaped fish, with white leading edges on its fins, made an enduring impression on me.

It happened west of Caroline during a family picnic on the Tay River, a small tributary of the Clearwater. I had snuck off from potato salad and chicken sandwiches, coupled with boring adult conversation, to clamber out on that logjam. The context is still clear. The logs had collected on an outside bank, pick-up-stick fashion, I suppose from a previous flood, maybe several. Some of the logs were white with age, the bark sloughing off them; other trees were fresh and you could get a good grip on them. The current spun around the corner and disappeared into a mesmerizing abyss beneath my feet.

Had my mother caught me there, words would have been spoken, followed by an obligatory swat or two. I suppose I was about 10, and at that age, the scale of water depth, danger and adventure was far out of proportion to adult sensibilities, especially maternal ones.

But I swear, that bull trout was as long as I was tall, or nearly so, it seemed to me. On that I am clear after nearly 60 years. I dropped my only lure, a Red & White Len Thompson, to dangle it in front of the trout's nose. My parents would have frowned at the idea of lure redundancy – having more than one hook in the tackle box. A lure was to be protected, stewarded and, if lost, retrieved. It was a gamble to present it to this fish, since it took some manoeuvring to get it down through the labyrinth of logs.

Mercifully, it did not bite out of hunger, boredom or anger, for the ensuing ride would have been unforgettable. The trout looked like it was suspended in air, the water was that clear; it hovered there, showing no interest in my lure or the predator perched above it. I was clearly no threat to this pinnacle of aquatic predators.

Even by 1960, this bull trout would have been a loner – a survivor of net, spear, set line and the occasional rifle bullet. Some people saw them not as sport fish but as "trash" fish unworthy of consideration by a refined angler. Others, in the process of rationalization, derided the predatory habits of bull trout while forgetting their own. Many just saw the trout as cheap protein, expendable by the washtub-full.

At that time, the Tay River still ran clean, clear and cold, through groves of mostly intact aspen, balsam poplar, willow and spruce. The transformation of the lower watershed with an agricultural blitzkrieg had only just begun. A juggernaut of logging, petroleum exploration and development with extensive road building was to follow. But no one saw the changes, or their additive impacts happening. The singular vision was to tame this wild land, civilize it and make it productive and profitable. If someone did see a connection between land-use change and the decline of native trout, it was dismissed as the price of progress.

As declines in native trout became evident, the answer, on the part of anglers and others, was to ignore the obvious and stock non-native fish, like brown trout and eastern brook trout, in the Tay River. As pristine habitat deteriorated, these imports initially prospered in the new disturbed habitat. Indiscriminate stocking of non-native trout gave the impression that humans could amend the laws of nature – we could have our development cake and eat it (and fish) too.

The combination of habitat loss and competition from non-native trout was (and is) particularly devastating for the bull trout, since the attack came from different but additive angles. The effects of new and multiple threats, applied simultaneously, are difficult or impossible to adjust to, or to survive. The preponderance of extirpation weaponry comes not from natural causes but from humans.

I was too young to see this, to understand consequences, and to voice a concern. There are no bull trout left in the Tay River to inspire memories. The blueprint for local extirpation was followed and completed. I can't go back to that logjam, or any other, to find a memory of my youth or an indicator of a different world, filled with possibilities. The bull trout of the Tay River are now ghosts.

But the memory of that bull trout of my youth is vivid and still resonates. In my mind hangs a picture of that trout, unclouded by the passage of time or the trivialities of living. Seeing it had a profound and long-lived impact on me. I can only hope someone will wave a recovery wand over the Tay River so that, someday, another kid will peer through a new logjam and be inspired by another bull trout.

LOVING FISH

It was a walk, unlike many others, that started a journey of discovery. Before that walk, I'd tried in vain to get people to love fish. I thought if we counted more and better, people would embrace fish. It didn't work! It's hard to be attracted to fish, existing as they do in an aquatic medium foreign to us terrestrial humans. Despite ever-increasing effort, awareness about fish remained low, and generally things continued to worsen for fish.

That's been the story of Alberta for over a hundred years. In the records of the NWMP post at Pincher Creek is an 1880s notation of concerns about declining fish populations. "If only we had been here a few years ago when fish were plentiful," wistfully wrote one of the officers. In subsequent decades, trout populations along the Eastern Slopes continued to decline precipitously; even historically high pike and walleye populations in Alberta's lakes were of concern. It wasn't a happy story for fish.

I asked myself, was the trend irreversible or was there hope for Alberta's aquatic residents? For me, the answer started as a walk across a pasture with Hilton Pharis. Hilton's grandfather "discovered" this place, now called Willow Valley, on a hunting trip. He was a settler on the prairies, where water was always in short supply. The valley, watered by Todd Creek and its springs, motivated him to resettle his family in these headwaters and establish the Elkhorn Ranch.

Sometimes our perception of the landscape does not mirror reality. The family albums of the Pharis family, with images from multiple generations, tell a story of succession, growth and prosperity. Also recorded, in the background of many photographs, are the changes to Willow Valley over time. Over the years, Hilton began to notice that willows were in short supply in this valley bearing their name.

Cutthroat trout had also declined. The trout used to spawn in the gravel riffles beneath the umbrella of willows, including by the ranch house. It was now harder to catch the occasional fish for supper. Warning signs were beginning to flash.

Taking stock of the ranch, the family set some goals for themselves: manage the water, the grass and the timber to ensure the ranch's success and the thriving of the more-than-human inhabitants – fish, wildlife and wildflowers. In that walk across the pasture, Hilton articulated his goal: "I want to leave the ranch better than I found it." I realized that my role was to help him help the fish.

Walking across the pasture with Hilton was the beginning of a new insight into how many ranchers and farmers feel about their land and what grows on it, walks across it or swims through it.

The business of the Elkhorn Ranch is raising cattle. For the Pharis family, raising cattle doesn't mean being blind to the rest of the ranch – its pieces and interrelationships. And maintaining fish means that you can't be blind to the watershed and what happens there; you can't be fish-centric, always peering into the water while ignoring the rest of the landscape.

That walk across the pasture with Hilton changed my perspective from being fish-centric to thinking broadly about the watershed. If we manage watersheds better, smarter and sooner, I reasoned, we reduce the cascade of issues, pulled down by gravity, that overwhelm the water, the people and the fish.

The Pharis family understood their responsibility for water and other shared resources, like fish. Their management of livestock and of the ranching operation circled back to the three basic goals. Off-stream water developments, streambank fencing, rotational grazing and selective logging all worked together in an interlocking mechanism related to water, grass and timber.

Their efforts have been multiplied by working with their neighbours to restore a watershed that is healthier, more productive and more resilient. Willows started to prosper, filling in some of the naked stream banks and restoring many of the riparian functions.

The stewardship efforts of the Pharis family began to catch the eye of others. A growing awareness in agricultural circles, beginning in the United States, led to recognizing riparian areas as extremely productive and valuable and not as "sacrifice" zones to be ignored. At the same time, knowledge about the wealth of ecosystem services provided by riparian areas began to surface.

Coincidentally, Alberta's beef industry had done some soul-searching through an independent audit of issues facing the industry. Riparian management was one of the issues identified. This began a conversation, starting around Hilton's kitchen table.

Many conversations later, a nongovernment stewardship initiative, called Cows & Fish, emerged, aided by the learnings from Willow Valley.

This grew into province-wide engagement and outreach, with presentations that identified what a riparian area is, since people may have seen them, crossed them, walked in them and even lived in them without recognizing their unique nature. They became aware that the green zones around lakes and wetlands, the emerald threads of vegetation that border rivers and streams, and the lush fringe in the valleys they flow through are riparian areas.

There was a growing realization that riparian areas run through our lives and livelihoods, just as the water that forms them runs through our bodies. Riparian-awareness messaging through Cows & Fish continues today, some 30 years later, building on thousands of interactions throughout communities and watersheds in Alberta.

Cutthroat trout spawn again in a riffle a stone's throw from Hilton and Alta's front door. Their grandkids occasionally catch a fish, startling both them and the fish. I hope they see fish like their parents and grandparents do, as a sign that the watershed is well. I have learned that it's not about loving fish, but about seeing fish as a vital component of the landscape, as are kids and willows and water.

TROUT LEANINGS

As if I were stalking a deer, my approach to the pool was slow and stealthy. The mountains rising from the valley and the stream had an ancient quality to them, and yet, as I threaded my way through the willow, spruce and alder, they appeared new and fresh to me. As I peeked over a downed spruce log into the pool, a trout – the trout – aligned itself, nose into the current, like a magnetic compass bearing.

Easing myself into the run at the end of the pool, I was instantly aware of the force of the current. Unlike a sleek trout, I felt more like a piece of plywood oriented perpendicular to the flow, and just as manoeuvrable. By comparison, the trout kept its position with effortless undulations of its tail, almost heedless of the current.

Water is denser by many times than air and is thus foreign territory to us air breathers. Being transported to Jupiter, where the pressure of the overlying atmosphere and the force of gravity is greater than Earth's, might provide a comparative for the crushing feeling of the aqueous atmosphere of trout habitat. It was in this wet crucible that trout took their forms, forged in a dense medium tumbling with the force of gravity, ever downward.

If trout were airplanes, they would be of the needle-nosed, svelte, ultra-manoeuvrable and fast, fighter jet variety. The tail is the equivalent of the jet engine, offering propulsion on demand as well as serving as a rudder. As the trout is propelled forward, the dorsal fin prevents it from rolling and yawing. Twinned pectoral fins prevent rolling and pitching; help the fish to turn; and, combined with the paired pelvic fins, provide braking power. As a drag racer, a trout's zero to 60 acceleration rate would be breathtaking, as is the ability to turn on a watery dime.

The patterns on the backs and sides of trout, the blushes of colour, the artful array of brilliant spots, are maps of a world at its beginnings, amid mountain building, glaciation and violent weather events. They, their kin and their ancestors were able to adapt to an environment of dramatic change, of chaos and of stunning variability. Trout have an ecological taproot thousands upon thousands of years old that anchors them to a landscape. Having survived so much, they are now at risk of having their essential landscape anchors swept away in an orgy of accelerating human land-use desires.

Trout are the oracles of their watersheds. Their presence, distribution, abundance and population viability provide both a wise and an insightful counsel, and a report card on our stewardship of watersheds. These same properties and their recent trends are also prophetic predictors of an impoverished future if we do not heed the silent messages from the trout.

Oblivious to me and the human world, the trout slipped silently under a root wad and remained there with only an occasional flick of a pectoral fin. From above, it was almost invisible, intricately camouflaged from avian predators. A grasshopper failed in its landward leap, falling short onto the surface of the pool. The ripples spread out from its struggles, telegraphing to the trout that something of interest had landed.

From its lair amid the roots, the trout rose slowly. I assumed it was to get the trigonometry right – distance, vector and differential velocities. Calculations completed, the muscular tail drove the trout upward, mouth open, like the maw from hell. The grasshopper disappeared into the void. The trout continued skyward, escaping into another medium momentarily, until burst speed was overcome by gravity.

With a mighty splash, the trout slapped the pool surface and darted into a rock cleft, out of the current. In due time, the grasshopper would become trout flesh, trout energy, trout memory.

Time passed and an aspen leaf floated by, not missed by the vigilant stare of the trout. Not a food item, not yet, but in the fullness of time, as the shredders dismantled it, the leaf would become the fuel for a caddisfly or a mayfly and then for a stonefly, all definitely trout food units.

This trout was large enough to have survived mergansers, kingfishers, osprey, mink and maybe even river otters. Beyond a certain size, the risk of being someone else's dinner declines. The trout rested on the bottom of the pool with only two motivations – food and seasonal sex.

In the cold water of that mountain stream, with winter ice cover persisting for months, metabolism slows, as does growth. That combination lends itself to a long lifespan for a fish that survives its youth. This trout, I reckoned, must have been an octogenarian in trout years.

Another grasshopper floated on the pool's surface. It had a different shape and drifted somewhat erratically, as though another trout had taken an unsuccessful bite at it. An easy meal is never something to be ignored, so the trout slowly rose to mid-pool depth to reconnoitre. There it stopped for a moment, pausing, ever so attentive to danger. You don't get big and old by neglecting caution. Sensing no danger, it accelerated and hit the grasshopper with full-bore enthusiasm.

But, after another skyward orbit, the trout found itself impaled at the end of an almost invisible monofilament line, unable to break free. The grasshopper was a fake, an artful rendition of the real thing, with a sharp hook hidden amid the wrapping of the fly. I admired the trout in my grasp – sleek, muscular and torsional. It was like hanging onto a writhing, greased and decompressing coil spring.

After having escaped many predators and enduring floods, drought, a forest fire, and sediment from logging clear-cuts and roads, the trout had fallen prey to a two-legged predator. Later that evening, I ate the trout, and just as the grasshopper had become part of the trout, the trout became part of me. As the stream flowed through the trout, it then flowed through me, binding and bonding me to both.

No longer do I kill native trout, whose range along the Eastern Slopes has shrunk. Populations have cratered, and all species are imperilled, whatever the scientific designation might be. I also cannot bear the thought of killing a trout, however inadvertently, with catch and release. Admittedly, I relax this principle for catching (and eating) non-native trout, many of which compete with their native cousins.

That does not stop me from walking beside or wading in a stream, seeing the surface shimmer and dimple with the energy of the current, hoping to see a trout rise to break the surface tension. In that I find enough joy, without the feeling of the tug of a trout at the end of a line. Although I miss the contest of angling in streams with wild native trout, I realize that, if catching fish were my only objective, I would miss so much more of the array around me.

I still find I can feel connected with trout and be continually inspired by observing them in the riffles, beneath the overhanging banks, tucked into root masses, and in the pools of transparently clear water. The way trout orient themselves, how they both resist and work with the current, their tenacity in the face of many odds, gives them a grace humbling to observe.

It is in those wooded valleys, with quiet beaver ponds, and the backbone of Earth exposed, where native trout still swim, that one is reminded of things older than humankind – of mystery and of humility.

Trout are the embodiment of all of the elements of a stream and its watershed, writ large by their presence. They are creatures that, once lost, cannot be put back together again – cannot be made right, populations restored, even with the wealth of a thousand mines.

Taxonomists place trout in rigid pigeonholes within the standard, Linnaean classification system. But some creatures are so emblematic of their environments that they might be placed in separate categories – based on uniqueness, symbolism and connectedness. For me, a biologist and an angler, trout occupy a separate place – a place of the heart.

5

Water: Not a Dry Subject

Thousands have lived without love,
not one without water.

— W. H. Auden

FOR THE LOVE OF A RIVER

We often say that we "love" our homes, cars etc. – and sometimes, even our jobs. We make this declaration because these things provide us with pleasure, comfort, pride or a sense of accomplishment. Can something incapable of being owned, something detached from our lives that is inanimate, unresponsive and obviously uncaring, be a focus for love? Can love be applied to a river?

What is a river? At first glance, a river is water, but water itself is the sum of many parts. Its beginnings include snow-melt and rain falling on absorbent surfaces created by intact habitats like forests and grasslands. Those drops of water channel into hundreds of small drainages, rivulets, runs, ravines and larger streams, collectively delivering the accumulated flow to a channel big enough to accommodate all of it. It needs saying that water doesn't come from a river, it first must come *to* a river. Only then does the river deliver water to us.

By the way, rivers are ill-defined. What is called a river in one place might be a stream or a creek in others. In Newfoundland, every bit of running water is a "brook," despite differences in size and flows. Like the waters to which the names are attached, definitions are fluid.

A river is a fractal network whose pieces, always moving from smaller to greater, are not divisible. There are no surplus parts or pieces of lesser priority, importance or significance. It is all together – or not at all. It is, in many ways, like the veins and arteries that form our circulatory system. You cannot exist on just part of your bloodstream.

The skeleton of a river is defined by its physical geography – bedrock, substrate and gradient. It is also a function of its geologic history, especially the action of past glaciers, which influence present-day channels. A river conforms to simple laws of gravity, friction and volume of water.

A river is water. It is defined by the amount of flow that fills its channel and the variation over seasons. The river's water moves over a channel bed that has been pushed, shoved and moulded by larger flows into undulations and irregularities, giving rivers a variety of configurations and water depths. Riffles, flowing over the humps in the river bottom, are the shallow, fast-flowing and noisy sections, while pools, collecting in the hollows, are the deep, slow and quiet portions.

In defiance of the straight geometry of our roads, fields and fences, a river is curvaceous, not adhering to straight lines and edges. It tugs endlessly at its banks, causing them to crumble in real and geologic time. Even on the insides of the curves, .

changing water levels can revise the riverbanks. Sometimes we build too near the edge and what we build crumbles too. We have yet to learn that, when we live on a bend in the river, we must bend with the river.

A river stirs the edge of a surveyed, manufactured world with a wildness of swirling eddies, soft backwaters, and a green confusion of banks. It is like a symphony playing across the land – small streams, small instruments, each of which can barely be heard, but gathered together, they make one voice. A voice that sings. A voice of music. Within the natural harmony, a beauty of form.

Listening to a river, it gurgles and chortles to itself in notes our ears can hear but we can barely interpret. A river sings to us and, sometimes, about us. It can roar with a ferocity that we can feel viscerally, and we are fearful of the message. It is equally frightening when a river goes quiet, as it does when flows drop to a low ebb. Deep down, we know the water that runs in the river also runs in us. A river's silence is a worrying signal, a sign that we need to act – and stop ignoring.

A musical score is a series of symbols arranged on lines that must be read to understand the composer's message. River music requires the same discipline – and the ability to read, interpret and comprehend the symphony of time, energy and diversity. Once acquired, the ability to read what the river tells us is a wonder.

When we can read the notes, hear the music, comprehend a river's architecture and appreciate its moods, a river becomes tangible, important – and we become bonded to it. Understanding a river, seeing its beauty, intricacy and diversity, is the pathway to loving it.

THE EASTERN SLOPES
Streams of Consequence

———

Snugged up against the bordering mountain chain of the Rockies, the Eastern Slopes of Alberta comprise a forested foothills and montane ecosystem of eastward-trending drainages that stretch from the US border to the boreal forest. Pinched to a thin wedge in the south, they widen to a numbing expanse of mostly coniferous forest to the north.

From north to south, east to west, the Eastern Slopes are an intricate, interactive, connected amalgam of creatures, biotic relationships, physical factors, geography, geology and ecological processes, coupled with history and accidents. The word *slopes* denotes a gradient, and down that incline, obeying the law of gravity, flows what the Eastern Slopes are mainly about – water.

Follow a river's flow upstream, past the farms, cities and industries, past the legislature, the sewage outfalls, over the dams, and finally into the Eastern Slopes. Up an ever-narrowing channel, following one of myriad channel choices, you will find a trickle of water where the river seems to start. It will never start in one place but in dozens, maybe hundreds, of trickles, meltwaters and rivulets splintering out in a spray of small water courses.

Headwater streams are small, often no wider than the length of your stride. In such streams, I have dammed the flow just by putting my boot across the tiny channel. They may have discontinuous flow for parts of the year, flowing underground for short distances before emerging through the gravel to be seen again. Some can be seasonal, running in spring during snowmelt but drying in summer when the rains wane.

There isn't a single term to describe them – they are trickles, dribbles, cricks, brooks, branches, runs, rills, rivulets. Hence the ambiguity about them. Not big enough often to have names, too small to be recognized, ignored as insignificant, and treated badly. Yet these headwater tributaries are the collectors, the accumulators and the initial conveyors of water that form streams with names.

Streams and rivers with names, with identities, don't spring forth fully formed, with channels brimming with water. They need help to reach that stature. All the little tributaries that form them, giving them prominence, need to be recognized.

Geographers categorize streams by "order" based on the relative size of the stream. The smallest tributaries are first-order streams, two first-order streams coalesce to form a second-order stream; and so on. About 80 per cent of the streams in the world are first- and second-order headwater streams.

These headwater streams often account for the greatest length of a watercourse in a watershed. The US Geological Service says that 60 per cent of stream length is composed of first-order streams and 20 per cent of second-order streams. Despite their invisibility, first- and second-order streams make up most of a watershed.

Many streams have been consistently overlooked as being fish-bearing, because, to the uninitiated, they seem too small to harbour fish. Yet they do. One stream in the Crowsnest Pass is tiny, a trickle to most eyes. But it contains native cutthroat trout. A "trophy" fish from this stream fits in the palm of my hand.

Because many headwater collectors lack continuous water, and are perceived as always ephemeral or dry, they miss out on protection from a variety of land uses. Small nondescript drainages are routinely cut over by loggers and truncated by roads.

In a clear, succinct systems description, author Norman Maclean wrote, "Eventually, all things merge into one and a river runs through it." Forest management in Alberta has a blind spot to this and fails to recognize that these streams merge into a larger, connected drainage network. Consequently, logged cutblocks routinely modify hydrologic response, producing faster snowmelt and greater runoff in the spring, followed by diminished flows later in the year. It's a case of too much water early, followed by too little later.

In a double whammy, because protective buffers are lacking or not wide enough, these little drainages are engulfed in sediment from logging operations, roading and subsequent off-highway vehicle use. All the sediment merges to pour into streams containing trout.

The lack of appropriate buffers on small streams is related to the economics of logging, but the omission is not justified by the science. Even the best buffer zones established on larger streams and rivers cannot improve conditions for fish or water quality when headwater streams are ignored. However well-intentioned, fighting gravity by only protecting lower stream reaches is a losing proposition. Starting at the top is the key to watershed protection.

The Eastern Slopes are the "trout heart" of Alberta. Bull trout, Westslope cutthroat trout, mountain whitefish, Athabasca rainbow trout (Alberta's only native rainbow) and Arctic grayling are the "natives," the ones whose tenure stretches back to the melting of the Laurentide and Cordilleran glaciers. However, the beat of that trout heart is waning. Now, it's not so much about the big one that got away, but rather the big one that isn't there anymore.

The rivers and streams of the Eastern Slopes are part of a landscape of water, plus forests, plus grizzlies and elk, plus native trout. In terms of conventional physical attributes, a native trout represents an infinitesimal fraction of the volume, discharge and energy flowing in streams and rivers. But subtract that trout and the whole watershed dies.

A closer look at Alberta's provincial coat of arms, especially the green divider between towering peaks and wheat fields, will reveal some flaws and scars. Set upon by many economic and recreational pursuits, the Eastern Slopes is now a patchwork of roads, dams, clear-cuts, mine pits, wellsites, pipelines and mud holes. The seeds of trout habitat destruction were sown through a variety of bad land-use decisions and sleeping government watchdogs.

Reckless logging, an excessive road network, and other incursions have put the Eastern Slopes through a shredder, turning clear streams murky with mud every time it rains. In watersheds not so impacted, streams continue to run clear, but we have so few pristine watersheds left to act as benchmarks that we take it as a given that rain equals muddy water.

If that isn't enough, we are missing an abundant winter snow-pack, which used to melt slowly, feeding rivers and streams and keeping water temperatures at a thermostat level that trout like. A slow melt under forest cover also translates into much of the water going into shallow groundwater, a subterranean reservoir, that keeps rivers flowing, even in winter when there is no runoff. For our trout, this is the essential thermal safety valve, the survival mechanism that allows them to weather the hot, bluebird days of summer. Climate change, giving us less snow and more rain (sometimes delivered torrentially), is an added bit of grief to struggling trout populations.

We are incrementally, cumulatively losing the essential functions of these headwaters, from which two out of every three Albertans derive their drinking water, and upon which two other provinces rely for that essential liquid. It isn't as if we haven't recognized the importance of the Eastern Slopes. Federal civil servants in the late 19th century recognized the pivotal role of the headwaters and set up the mechanism for delineating the Eastern Slopes for watershed protection. Subsequent governments mouthed the words and even enshrined the words in policy. But in fine print were the words "No legitimate proposals will be categorically rejected." This was, of course, code for "The Eastern Slopes are open for business."

It has always been government policy to protect the Eastern Slopes; it's just that it has never been government practice to do so. The process follows the Law of Inverse Relevance – the less you intend to do about something, the more you have to keep talking about it. And we have talked through iterations of East Slopes Policy, Integrated Resource Plans and, more recently, the Land Use Framework, with its suite of regional and subregional plans. The outcomes have been the division of the Eastern Slopes into zones. Mining here, grazing there, logging almost everywhere, resort development, and a few specks of landscape with (so far) no economic interest set aside for protection. As Aristotle commented some 23 centuries ago, "What is common to the greatest number has the least care bestowed upon it."

Multiple use has led to multiple abuse. Ultimately, what will save the Eastern Slopes, with its array of native trout, grizzlies, caribou, wolverine, limber pine and other more-than-human life? Sometimes it feels like we are swimming against the flow of economic determinism in the Eastern Slopes. We need to make room in our economic aspirations for an Eastern Slopes of space, quiet and integrity.

The answer will be found in the vigilance and persistence of believers – people who will not accept the premise that the Eastern Slopes is a warehouse open for ransacking. It will be people who have a connection, or who are learning of their connection, to the headwaters. Those people will understand that water runs downhill from the headwaters to them, and what happens in the watershed not only affects the water they drink but also increases the risk of flood waters in their basements.

They will appreciate space with ecological integrity, even though many may never go there. These people will have developed literacy in matters ecological. They will recognize that native fish – their presence, distribution and abundance – are an indicator of watershed and landscape health. They will come from the ranks of the public; industry; the civil service; and local, provincial and federal politicians.

Izaak Walton, the author of *The Compleat Angler*, published in 1653, quoted an unnamed "ingenious Spaniard" in that famous tome: "Rivers and the inhabitants of the watery elements are made for wise men to contemplate and for fools to pass by without consideration." The same sentiment can be applied to the Eastern Slopes.

WHAT'S A WETLAND WORTH?

———

It wasn't much of a pond – more like a puddle, in some minds. Most called it a slough, a somewhat demeaning term. It filled up in the spring and slowly receded into a sea of foxtail by late summer. Runoff from a small watershed of aspen forest, pasture and farmland fed the pond. Once the pond had more water and an outlet, but road ditches diverted much of the flow to other routes.

As I remember it, as summer progressed, a patina of duckweed and algae developed. Mosquitoes swarmed out of it, to be met with ferocious dragonflies, the helicopter gunships of the insect world. An olfactory aura surrounded the pond – rich, earthy and often breathtaking. No cropland was harmed by its spreading waters, and the loss of pasture was compensated for by a shorter walk for the cows to water and a band of lush, tall grass ringing the pond, hidden water quenching the thirst of their roots.

Willows surrounded the pond in a near-perfect doughnut, sinking their roots into the saturated soil, and aspen flanked them in the drier upland. The dead aspen among them were light enough for a boy to move and assemble into a raft. Dead aspen is more a sponge than a buoyant material, so the voyages were short and always culminated in wet feet, if not other body parts. I yearned for better materials to undertake longer voyages of discovery.

Much of the human body is water, about 65 per cent. The rest is just framing, plumbing and wiring. It is said that people born on coasts are subject to an irresistible pull back to water. "The ocean has an old allure," they say, "to draw her exiles back."

Since all life began in the primordial soup of ancient oceans, it's not surprising that we have some sort of genetic hardwiring to succumb to that allure.

Even prairie-born and -raised people display that attraction to water. Whether it was hardwiring, desperation or intrigue, the pond drew me as a kid like no other part of the farm. It also drew the first wave of ducks, mostly mallard drakes, with the unmistakable metallic sheen to their heads. Every so often, in the early mists of morning, one could catch a glimpse of a deer drinking at its margins. A garter snake, surging out of the grass beneath one's feet, generally got the pulse rate racing.

Swallows collected mud from the pond edges for their nests built under the eaves of the barn. A cacophony of birdsong filled the air: wrens scolding, warblers proclaiming that their perch was the best, and a red-tailed hawk pair who vocally resented each intrusion into their neighbourhood. Yellow birds, gray birds, brown birds and multicoloured birds. I wasn't to learn the theory until much later, but I knew that if I wanted to see wildlife, the pond was the place. We know now that riparian areas harbour a disproportionately large share of Canada's wildlife; that is part of their allure.

Someone with a strong arm could throw a rock across my wetland, and at its deepest, a person of medium height could have waded through with impunity. However, to a small boy, its size, depth and workings were unfathomable.

The pond provided the auditory signal of spring, brought by chorus frogs. At our place, it wasn't spring, officially, until their trills were heard. Observing the males with their impossibly inflated sac required stealth and patience. An occasional great blue heron taught me those attributes. The transformation of egg clumps to tailed larvae and then to adults was an independent lesson in biology, but where did they go when the pond dried up?

And what creatures made those other swamp noises? Investigation, tinged with a bit of fear, revealed that the pond also had leopard and wood frogs. It was while I crouched at twilight to observe these other creatures that an orange sunset, reflected and framed in the water, found a permanent home in my memory.

So what is a wetland like that worth? Economically, it's hard to put a price tag on it, although we are getting better at valuing the significant ecological goods and services that wetlands provide. Could we do without wetlands? No! Beyond all the things we now know that wetlands contribute, that pond provided me with an education, experiences, risks, inspiration, entertainment, connections and a sense of wonder. It was like thousands scattered through central Alberta and across the prairies. Most are now gone.

How many do we need? As we are slowly beginning to appreciate, most of them. Climate change has begun to sensitize us to wetland values. Wetlands hold and store water against drought and dampen the effect of floods. Their potential to filter, buffer and improve water quality is impressive. Maintaining, restoring and appreciating wetlands should be the path we diligently follow. My pond is still there, and it is priceless.

A PAEAN AND A PLEA FOR PRAIRIE RIVERS

————

Black. Malevolent, ominous black. Filling the sky, moving on a dramatically rising wind came a cloud so inky black it seemed like you could dip a quill pen in it and write a story. The story that was written had short, breathless chapters. The temperature plummeted, and the warm breeze became an icy blast. Gale-force winds quickly picked up our two Kevlar canoes, each laden with two 20-kilogram jugs of fresh water, and hurled them a hundred metres end over end in the air. We watched in a combination of amazement and angst as we grimly held onto our kitchen shelter, which flapped and buckled in the breeze like an untended sail.

A prairie river short story, over in minutes, with a mostly happy ending. The canoes, after experiencing flight, landed on shore with a few extra scratches and minor dents. A tarp was shredded, poles were bent, and heart rates accelerated. This was not a coastal hurricane but a prairie river setting, where one learns to expect a surprising catalogue of weather events.

Life is not a soap opera. There is no written script for the day. Things happen on a river where high banks can obscure impending events, and within minutes, one can be jolted from smoking hot to the chill of a cascade of hail. Lightning stabbing down is Nature's fireworks, but it can seem less entertaining than electrifying, especially while paddling in an aluminum canoe or camped beneath a tall cottonwood. An overnight rain shower can cleanse and freshen the air, sharpening the sense of smell, especially for coffee percolating and bacon frying.

Prairie rivers can be in flood, leaving you dodging floating battering rams in the form of large cottonwood tree trunks. Or they can have water levels so low that you spend your day scraping over sandbars and hopping out often to drag the canoe as river levels drop to trickles. You can be sailing along downstream, barely dipping your paddle, making over ten kilometres an hour or, a few minutes later, putting your shoulder to an upstream wind, with metre-high waves seeming to reverse the river's flow and any slackening of effort leaving you propelled backwards.

These rivers keep you mentally and physically alert and active as they see-saw from capricious to constant, unpredictable to boring, and mundane to sublime.

The thin band of riparian green, often only a few metres wide, is a magnet for biodiversity, supporting everything from cottonwoods to kingbirds. Mornings, under a canopy of cottonwoods, are a cacophony of birdsong. Gray catbirds meow, yellowthroats sing a distinctive "witchety-witchety-witchety," and the mourning doves, well, they sound plaintively mournful. One evening, just after dark, a herd of elk stampeded past our camp, disturbed (maybe annoyed) by our presence at their watering place. Beavers slapped their tails, alerting their family to interlopers on shore.

Prairie river valleys can have abrupt cliff faces with ironstone caprocks shoring up erodible sandstones and shales. In these sheltered nooks and crannies, prairie and peregrine falcons nest, their insistent cries a signal of our trespass. Eroded badlands, a tortured landscape often replete with the fossilized remains of bizarre creatures long missing from Earth, give way to uplands of flat to undulating native grasslands (or grasslands converted to fields of canola or wheat).

Ironically, you are on water, and you might think *Water, water everywhere*, but there is not a drop for you to drink: too many upstream pipes disgorging our wastes, coupled with agricultural runoff and livestock manure flushed into the river, mean that hauling drinking water with you on a prairie river float is a necessity.

Prairie rivers are also the recipients of all the sediment eroded from upstream sources. There are times when these rivers seem too thick to drink, too thin to plow. Mudbanks can become not only sole sucking, as in wrenching off your sandals or rubber boots, but also soul sucking, for the intense effort required to move. We once used the truck's winch to drag our canoes 50 metres through a particularly gluey, viscous stretch at a take-out point.

River access points are few and far between, which means a prairie river trip will be a multiday voyage, not something for those in a hurry. The benefit is an immersion into the ebb and flow of these rivers, as we are swept along. Flowing water has an ancient rhythm and an inexorable power to transform landscapes. Sometimes, recognizing these qualities requires observation and reflection.

With days to spend, it is not a race but a relaxing luxury to absorb the river, its valley and the inhabitants. It is time well wasted. Sitting quietly, you can hear the rush of the nighthawk's wings as it swoops to collect (hopefully) a biting insect. A walk might, for the observant, disclose a couple of cryptically coloured nighthawk eggs, laid on a bed of old gravels next to a teepee ring of rounded rocks. A fat bull snake, sunning on an outcrop, reluctantly squeezes itself into a crack in the rock to retain some privacy. Towards fall, when Canada geese are queuing up for migration, the quiet of a full-moon night might be shattered with constant goose music as they pile into quiet backwaters, disturbing those already slumbering.

Away from our temperature-moderated homes and vehicles, the vagaries of weather become intimate. It can be a somewhat less than subtle reminder of how close we live to the edge of survival. An unrelenting summer sun can bake you. Under a cottonwood canopy, the shade and slightly higher humidity is a welcome, cool refuge. As evening comes and the sun dips, you grab a sweater. The dew and chill of morning dissipates with a warming sun.

Whether under a filmy nylon tent fly or fully clothed in Gore-Tex, it is a pleasure to live with the weather, to feel the cool of rain or the warmth of the sun. You start to watch the sky with more concentration and speculate on the meaning of meteorological phenomenon. If your weather prognostication is correct, you will be in camp under the fly when the storm hits. A wrong guess and icy water will be running off your nose as you plot a course through a wave-chopped channel.

On the water, a few dragonflies skim the surface looking for prey. On shore, we become the go-to meal for no-see-ums, mosquitoes and biting flies. Thumbnail-sized horse- and deer-flies jab a blunt proboscis, like a fork tine, into you to start the blood flow. Uncovered and unprotected by strong bug dope, exposed skin takes on a red mottled appearance from swollen bites, giving the impression of a smallpox victim. Then the itching starts. Mesh screening seems like the best-ever invention, and inside these refuges from biting insects, a silent vote of thanks is given to the innovator.

So why sing the praises of places where the bugs can be murderous, the water undrinkable, the flows unpredictable, the storms monumental – not to mention the mud? Why return time and time again to such trepidation and torture?

Did I mention the expansive skies, often deep blue with puffy cumulous clouds? It could be the spaciousness and wildness of the landscape, which can humble our tendencies of hubris and control. Under night skies, with jillions of stars, we recall when this was a primary form of entertainment, seeking form and purpose in the illimitable void of space. A full moon provides a staircase of light on the water, giving rise to the idea that there is a heaven at its end. Lichen-covered stone structures remind us of Indigenous civilizations preceding ours, peoples who lived in harmony with these landscapes. There are coyote orchestras, toad arias and the rustling of cottonwood leaves in a breeze. All are counterpoints to human noise and infinitely more calming. Nowhere else does a beer, a can of beans and a slice of watermelon taste so good.

Most importantly, it is about being propelled by a flow not of our own design or speed and resigning ourselves to something more basic. In our increasingly complex digital age, a prairie river float is decidedly analog. It is about slowing our frenetic pace to Earth time, giving us pause to observe, reflect and be inspired. A float on a prairie river, like any wilderness adventure, is about reminding ourselves of elements larger than us and not within our control. Exposing ourselves to a bit of vulnerability is a step towards humility. Humans could stand a bit more humility, especially in our treatment of the natural world.

Economists always talk of substitutes, alternatives to resource gaps left by overexploitation. I've tried to imagine an alternative to a prairie river trip. Would it be to canoe down an irrigation canal, attempt to birdwatch beside a reservoir, and camp in a crowded, artificial riparian area complete with power, running water and flush toilets? I doubt anyone would be moved to sing the praises of those experiences or come home with such rich memories, bug bites and all. None of that rivals a trip down a prairie river.

Unfortunately, prairie rivers are out of sight and out of mind to most, including governments. Anything meeting those criteria is at risk.

Much of the flow of prairie rivers is licensed for removal, mostly for irrigation agriculture. This means that less water stays in these rivers, so that floating a canoe becomes more problematic and more paint is left on river rocks from scraping bottom. Failure to set appropriate instream flow needs for the aquatic environment, riparian area persistence, and recreation could force prairie rivers to spiral down to puddles of waste water.

Prairie rivers are a public resource, including for recreation, but no one in government seems to advocate for this use. Pressure continually mounts for more water withdrawals, without assessments of how diminished flows, coupled with climate change effects, would influence recreational use of these rivers and their ecological health. Treating water in rivers as a fungible commodity to be removed, rather than an ecological necessity to be retained, leaves prairie rivers struggling for existence. The World Wildlife Fund, in the 2009 report *Canada's Rivers at Risk*, included the South Saskatchewan River, a premier prairie paddling river, as one of ten Rivers at Risk in Canada because of low flow concerns.

As flows are reduced, water quality issues ratchet up. This creates serious impediments for native fish species, many of which are only found in prairie rivers. Lake sturgeon, a river-dwelling species, is an antediluvian survivor categorized as Threatened in Alberta and Endangered federally. Although rarely seen, even by anglers, these fish are every bit as much a part of these prairie landscapes as are rattlesnakes, short-horned lizards and brown thrashers.

As flows and water quality decline, invasive fish species like Prussian carp will increase. These "frankenfish" can survive extreme environmental conditions that native species can't. They can reproduce asexually using sperm from native minnow species and thus can outcompete our native prairie fish species assemblage. Though largely unseen, this aquatic invasion is akin to the terrestrial landscape being engulfed by Russian olive, leafy spurge and cheatgrass.

As in so much of the natural world where we find respite, recreation and rejuvenation, threats abound, mostly of our own making. Prairie rivers are at risk, like the grasslands through which they flow. They desperately require attention, oversight and respect. These prairie treasures need friends, supporters and defenders to advocate for their recreational attributes and their ecological health. They need them now, for the sky is ominous and darkening.

WHOSE WATER IS IT ANYWAY?

My introduction to the room full of irrigators by the District Agriculturalist was hardly cordial or collegial. In his mind, and in theirs, I was there to throw an unwanted environmental wrench into irrigation expansion plans along a small watershed mostly on the east side of the Porcupine Hills. It was a trial by fire for a young biologist.

Amid constant interruptions and heckling, I tried to make the point that the remnant trout in the creek needed water too. They needed the right amount of water – not all the water, but some, so they could get on with their life-cycle requirements. In many ways, the argument was similar to that of the irrigators – water is required for life. Despite my attempts to paint a similar perspective, in their view, it didn't wash. I was an impediment to their plans.

When I had finished my presentation to a chorus of boos, one irrigator stood up and proclaimed it was their (expletive deleted) water, not the (expletive deleted) trout's water. Furthermore, I was clearly biased, and why a government employee was so negative to them would be explored with their elected representative (a time-worn threat). What they needed were team players for irrigation, not me.

The irony of the assertion of bias wasn't lost on me, although it seemed so for them, oriented as they were solely for irrigation. To my relief, a tall, broad-shouldered individual stood up and told the crowd to quiet down. His demeanour (and size) commanded some attention, and quiet descended. He proceeded to point out that he was pleased I was biased, for just as they were biased in favour of expanded irrigation, he favoured the trout. As an angler, he wanted a government biologist to speak up, to advocate on behalf of the trout, and for the irrigators to recognize that other values were at stake in their expansion scheme.

It was a rare moment of support in front of an antagonistic audience (one of many in my career). Occasionally I roll that memory out to muse over. The irrigator group were somewhat cowed, and only a few muted grumblings remained. Later, I was to meet my benefactor, John Eisenhauer, as he formed the first chapter of Trout Unlimited Canada in Alberta.

The learning I took from that fractious meeting was that being a champion for trout, for instream flow needs – indeed, for suggesting a share of water be set aside for biodiversity reasons – is viewed by many as biased, rather than as standing for fairness and equity. Attempts to educate, engage and find reasonable solutions are stymied when those across the table hold all of the cards – or in this case, most of the water.

In the narrow irrigation paradigm held by those at the meeting, if you're not for irrigation, you must be against it. There is no middle ground. But nothing is that simple.

I don't live in such a black-and-white world. Like timber harvest, oil and gas development, urban expansion and other land uses, irrigation agriculture is an important economic generator for Alberta. But, like other land uses, if it's an all-or-nothing proposition, the end result is winners and losers, a fracture that fails to find some harmony between competing interests. More does not make Alberta better, because more of something means less of something else. More alfalfa, less trout.

Drying up the stream to raise more alfalfa might seem to be a perfectly acceptable thing to do if the place you get your mail is next to the hayfield. In the case of the irrigators in the room, it wasn't that they lacked access to water. They already had licences for water withdrawal, guaranteed through water rights. These were conferred through an ancient piece of legislation, in place before Alberta became a province. This created, for irrigators, an assured claim on water through something called "first in time, first in right."

I made it clear that I wasn't recommending a roll-back in water rights – those were legally entrenched. They already had dibs on most of the water in the stream. But they wanted more, and more meant the trout would be left high and dry, literally. The irrigators' view of rights did not involve obligations, especially to our fellow aquatic travellers.

Although government water managers have consistently failed to rein in irrigation interests, the fact is that water is a public resource in short supply, and it needs to be shared in such a way that instream uses and downstream users are minimally impacted. That requires an assessment of needs, which are then translated into flows. Those recommended flow amounts may vary throughout the year, but no one user should predominate at the expense of all other uses and users, including irrigation interests.

A paraphrase of the Golden Rule, "Do unto those downstream as you would have those upstream do unto you," sums it up nicely. Those living in Alberta's headwaters have not only rights but also obligations to downstream people and provinces. Downstream of the irrigators and their wishes for expansion were the expectations of residents of Lethbridge, then Medicine Hat, Prince Albert, Nipawin, The Pas, the Saskatchewan River Delta and finally Lake Winnipeg (with points in between). A lot of sharing is required, especially as flows decrease with climate change.

Just as there are economic thresholds that define the viability of a farm, so too are there ecological thresholds that mean the life, or death, of fish and the aquatic environment. If we can't get beyond the no man's land of greed – the mantras of "get all you can get" and beyond "me, me, me, and to hell with you" – then you can kiss all the other values of streams good-bye, including lush riparian areas, abundant fish and wildlife, and cherished natural amenities.

It seemed like that was just what that group of irrigators were prepared to do. In the same breath, all would have said they were good stewards, but in their minds, stewardship included not "wasting" the water by allowing it to flow downstream by and through a fish.

The rudimentary instream flow I recommended was finally accepted by the provincial water managers. But it was a pyrrhic victory, and too little, too late to save the dwindling trout population. Chronic overallocation, habitat loss and drought had an inescapable cumulative effect.

The stunning aspect is how quickly trout, an indicator of watershed integrity, disappeared. In the Glenbow Museum's photographic archive, I found an old black-and-white image of three anglers on the lower portion of this stream. The year was 1902, and they proudly held the results of a day's fishing – nearly 20 kilograms of Westslope cutthroat trout. Subsequently, in one human lifespan, native cutthroat trout yielded to introduced rainbow trout, and then the rainbows were gone.

This interaction with a group of irrigation farmers happened in the early part of my career. As I was to learn, questioning any of the tenets of irrigation was viewed as heresy, far worse than farting in church. Is there now a more enlightened position on the part of the irrigation sector? Sadly, it seems as entrenched now as in my early experience.

Later developments – a diversion structure upstream and construction of a new storage reservoir, all paid for by Alberta taxpayers – served the interests of the irrigators well. None of it benefited the now missing trout. So whose water was it? You can draw your own conclusions, since I am biased.

6

A Line in the Sand

*If the creator has a purpose in equipping us
with a neck, he surely would have meant
for us to stick it out.*

— Arthur Koestler

IF ONLY WE HAD THE EYES TO SEE
A Line in the Sand for Conservation

———

E.B. White, author of *Charlotte's Web,* must have been thinking about biologists when he said, "I arise in the morning torn between a desire to save the world and a desire to savor the world. That makes it hard to plan the day."

Being a biologist can be quixotic, akin to an Alice-in-Wonderland existence. To paraphrase the Red Queen, "You can have conservation yesterday or tomorrow, but not today." In that context, Lewis Carroll might have understood the fantasy of having both endless development and a healthy environment.

Maybe there is a mythical place, fuelled by this fantasy, where this unlikely combination exists, but rest assured, it is not Alberta – at least, not yet. Here, whenever we come up to the line in the sand, we scratch another line in the sand and continue on, oblivious to the implications of this madness. It's a blueprint for ecological self-destruction.

Former US vice-president and now ecological crusader Al Gore observed with substantial candour:

> We are in an unusual predicament as a global civilization. The maximum that is politically feasible, even the maximum that is politically imaginable right now, still falls short of the minimum that is scientifically and ecologically necessary.

But there is a chance, albeit thin, that we will pull out of our ecocidal dive. It might yet happen, based on some of the stories of exemplary individual efforts, the stewardship activities of concerned landowners and the dedicated efforts of biologists fighting hard, uphill battles with industry, and often with their employer, the government. It may happen because the market dictates it, based on a growing phenomenon called "social licence," where governments and industry increasingly need and are given approval by us, the voters and consumers, for their existence and business.

Biologists work in an often surreal world, with skeptics to the right, nonbelievers to the left, whiners behind and over-expectant enthusiasts ahead. Across years of study and work, of small successes and slow failures, of brief delights and long irritations, I have come to some conclusions about being a biologist. One is, as Yeats observed about the Irish, that we have an abiding sense of tragedy that sustains us through temporary periods of joy.

Part of the challenge is the persistence of the very human characteristics of ignorance, apathy, greed and blindness, the latter best described as false optimism. We define ourselves not by who we are but by what we drive, the square footage of our homes, and the toys arrayed around us. As individuals, the most terrifying four words we might hear are "You have a growth." Yet when applied to the province, the nation, growth is the goal.

We are living an ecological Ponzi scheme dominated by rampant resource extraction, especially nonrenewable forms, fuelled by an ideology that insists the economy is not only important but the only important thing. In many ways, we are not far removed from an economy fuelled by buffalo hides and tongues. Little thought is paid to consequences. It is simply capitalism working itself out in the exploitation of another available, profitable natural resource.

While arguments can be made for environmental protection from the angles of economics, risk management and missed or lost opportunities, ultimately the desire to save the Earth and all of its intricate, interlocked systems and processes must come from the human heart. What doesn't appeal to us cerebrally can draw us viscerally. It is there, in the heart, that truth resides.

The special magic of biology – or more to the point, ecology – lies in the ability to take organisms at a variety of scales and gain an understanding of their context, or habitat, that has meaning and a connection for us. Many of us humans think we live apart from our wild cousins; we are aided by our technology, our tools and the seemingly abundant supplies of stored sunshine in the form of petroleum. The role and the unstated objective of biologists is to remind us, unceasingly, that we live apart from the rest of the natural world only in our minds.

Any particular generation is seldom capable of foreseeing the lingering effects of its labours, but there are always a few survivors and observers who, at some point in their lives, are capable and have the chance to look back over their shoulders at what has been gained or lost.

These people can see clearly our passage and know that it is without a unifying plan for the future. They know well the adage "If you don't know where you're going, any road will take you there." It may be an undesirable destination, despite the cries of business-oriented leaders who swear that theirs is the path to enlightenment. Their light seems artificial, selfish and short term.

George Orwell might have been thinking about biologists and their truths when he said: "If liberty means anything at all, it means the right to tell people what they do not want to hear." At the very least we have an obligation to bear witness.

Robin Wall Kimmerer, an Indigenous botanist, writes in *Braiding Sweetgrass*, "We may not have wings or leaves, but we humans do have words. Language is our gift and our responsibility." Sadly, scientists have trouble conveying messages in words that engage the lay reader. This has real and profound consequences. If the public cannot discern the truths of scientific inquiry, how can they be informed and act upon them? Part of writing about science is being a translator. Effective translation helps people to open their eyes to see, to better employ their ears to hear, and to rejuvenate the capacity to feel.

The trend towards ecological literacy is slow and incremental. Our words tend to be overwhelmed by our consumer habits. We know where the dots are; we just don't seem to be able to connect them. It is distressing to be able to contribute very little to the ability of individuals and communities to make appropriate decisions – to see what is happening around us.

Sometimes, as a biologist with much experience, I feel pain when I think too much about what we do to landscapes and wild creatures. Perhaps it is better not to think but only to look – to see and to report. Edward Abbey, that caustic iconoclast, pointed out, "Love of wilderness is an expression of loyalty to the earth, the earth which bore us and sustains us, the only home we shall ever know, the only paradise we ever need – if only we had the eyes to see." And as the wise Pete Seeger said, "The world is going to be saved by people saving their own homes."

DELUSIONS OF CONSERVATION

For too long, we have listened and succumbed to the boilerplate of the federal and provincial government (and industry) telling us that all is well. The environment is in good hands. There is nothing to worry about. The fish are fine, except for the sores, growths and concentrations of heavy metals, pesticides and synthetic hormones; the water is drinkable, but don't touch it until it has been extensively and expensively treated; the air is as fresh as downtown Beijing's; wildlife is abundant, especially sparrows and starlings; and the viewscape is enhanced by all the marvelous artifacts of the development and engineering mind. Oh, and the noise is the symbol of progress, as is the lack of free space.

Reluctantly I have concluded that many of my fellow citizens have spent too much time smoking hopium. This seems especially true of politicians who say they support conservation; they are maintaining fish and wildlife populations; they care about watershed integrity and ensuring that basic ecosystem processes continue.

Hopium is – I assume, since I have never taken a puff – a magical, addictive drug that allows those who imbibe to really, really hope that the mindless, frantic pace of economic development will be balanced by some caring, ecologically sensitive counterweight. It is part of the dopiod family of reality-suppressing narcotics, similar to crystal meth, and it is one that effectively results in hypnotic death.

One of the consequences of smoking too much hopium isn't craving for junk food but rather embarking on a boat trip down the River of Forgetfulness. On this voyage, you become immune to reality, and everything you are told by bureaucrats, politicians and corporate spin doctors becomes believable, soothing and comfortable.

Before the fog of exploitive amnesia takes over, it would be good to read the words of Aldo Leopold. Writing in 1943 in the *Journal Of Wildlife Management*, he said:

> Our tools improve faster than we do. It is unlikely that economic motives alone will ever teach us to use our new tools gently. The only remedy is to extend our system of ethics from the man-man relation to the man-earth relation. We shall achieve conservation when and only when the destructive use of land becomes

unethical – punishable by social ostracism. Any experience that stimulates this extension of ethics is culturally valuable. Any that has the opposite effect is culturally damaging.

So the pathway suggested by Leopold for conservation might resemble the passage of a goat through a boa constrictor – highly visible and uncomfortable for all participants. Leopold, of course, speaks for the future, the manner in which we plan for tomorrow, and for the children of tomorrow. The way we currently plan is, despite the rhetoric, for today, following the economic imperatives of the short term. We leave the future to our children, for them to figure it out, without an ethical course to follow and possibly with them cursing us a few decades down the road.

Being in the throes of a resource exploitation boom isn't so different from an addiction to some mind- and body-altering substance. There's the denial that things are out of control; there's the frantic, frenetic lifestyle, the moral carelessness and the realization you're doing something you know isn't good for you, but you can't stop. Eventually, you collapse despite the reality-altering substances.

The thing about collapses – of ecosystems, civilizations and individuals – is that it never happens according to a plan. No slavering hordes of zombies, no blinding flash of nuclear war, no asteroid bumping us from the cosmos. No, the end doesn't usually come with a bang. It arrives with a set of virtually indistinguishable whimpers. Water becomes scarcer and harder to make potable. Food prices creep up because of loss of farmland, fertility and transport costs. Driving becomes a luxury based on fuel costs. There is no birdsong to remind us of our beginnings and associations. And, before we know it, we are squabbling over pieces of firewood and stone tools.

Until we wean ourselves from this pernicious drug of hopium, no change, other than the inevitable slide to landscape degradation, will occur. John Maynard Keynes, the famous British economist whose profession is often the least likely place to turn for wise advice, said, "The difficulty lies not in new ideas, but in escaping from the old ones." Good one, John.

It's time to clear our heads of the delusion of conservation. We need to trust our eyes, our brains and the measurements of objective science. It's difficult to look into the swirling, molten pit of endless material progress and not be mesmerized. The myth of growth is based on blinding hubris and an empire of illusion, of economics being the only metric, and technological panaceas providing the escape clause. It's time to overcome our hopium addiction and face reality, as difficult as that might be.

SQUEEZING THE TUBE

———

Just this morning, I squeezed the last glob of toothpaste from the tube. I know what you're going to say: "There is always a bit more left!" It is that mindset that keeps us squeezing the tube called Earth, assured that there is still more available. This is optimism bias – the natural tendency to underestimate what could go wrong.

Of course, if we employ strata-cracking fracking technology, we can eke out a bit more petroleum from the tube. We can suck a bit more water from diminishing river flows for another shopping centre, subdivision or potato field. One more road, mine or clear-cut shouldn't hurt bull trout, woodland caribou or grizzlies. Squeezing the tube continues unabated.

Our current economy is designed to squeeze the tube, hard, to create wealth. It has led to what economists call "a perpetual cornucopia machine," emptying one resource tube after another. The process requires a continual substitution as one tube after another runs dry. It is hardly perpetual, but it is all-consuming. The cost of wealth extraction creates devastating social, ecological and economic dilemmas that we ignore at our peril.

Even the most determined tube squeezer has to admit that, at a certain point, there is no more toothpaste. One might hope there is, as I did this morning for my ablutions. Hope is the last thing left in Pandora's Box, after everything else is emptied. We have a wonderful and endless capacity to believe in contradictions, like the existence of more full resource tubes despite evidence to the contrary.

Unlike my empty toothpaste tube, which I can replace with a full one, many of Earth's resources are not as apt to be easily replenished. Consider how many passenger pigeons are left in the greater tube called Earth. Where would one go to replace species now extinct? Unfortunately, the *Whole Earth Catalog* does not offer any new, whole Earths, or even replacement parts. If you think time will change the outcome, don't wait too long, for you will come to the realization, as I did, that the tube is empty.

THE LINGERING SMELL OF GASOLINE

———

William James, an American philosopher, once described a man who, whenever he was under the influence of laughing gas, knew the secret of the universe but always forgot it upon coming to. Finally, with immense effort, he wrote down the secret before the vision had faded: "A smell of petroleum prevails throughout."

Many in Alberta cling to February 13, 1947, when Imperial's Leduc No. 1 roared into existence, after the company had drilled 133 dry-hole wells throughout the province. Leduc No. 1 spewed oil over a farm field and thus began an era, decades long, of resource wealth. This was an accident of geology and jurisdiction for Alberta rather than any inspiration of human genius. The era begun by Leduc No. 2 is past its peak and may be passing quickly, as we connect the dots between petroleum use, greenhouse gas emissions and the severe implications of climate change. Use of renewable energy sources, in the form of wind and solar, may be the essential coffin nails for what remains of the Cretaceous Age.

Yet many will mourn the passing of this fossil fuel era, seeing its end as the province's great tragedy. Of course, it *is* a tragedy, but perhaps not the one its adherents have in mind. As the bumper stickers used to declaim, "Please God, if you give us another boom, we promise not to piss it away." Many hope against hope that another reawakening of the industry will bring back the outrageously high wages for high school dropouts, another sales spike for recreational vehicles and other adult toys, and further delay in federal and provincial politicians enacting the type of appropriate tax regime to effectively underwrite and sustain essential public services.

Petroleum brought wealth to Alberta's backwaters and to its skyscraper-shaded streets. Billions of dollars of investment poured in, creating a magnet for thousands of new Albertans and for many who came to make a financial killing but not a life. Petroleum transformed Alberta from a rural, agrarian economy to an urban one of technology, finance, manufacturing and services. Like the mushroom cloud of a nuclear blast, the transition happened at breakneck speed. The impact, like a wildfire, was unpredictable, spotty and momentarily devastating.

Unnoticed was the wealth that poured out of the province, in the form of unprocessed, underprocessed and unrefined petroleum products. It was said, by some, that if you held your ear to the ground you could hear the wealth being sucked out of Alberta. But few listened. Instead of transitioning from the traditional hewers of wood and drawers of water, we merely substituted the giveaway of other natural resource products. This was done under the stated but dubious tenet that the petroleum industry was the great generator, after all, of all the good we had come to expect. Diversification of our economy to give us a more realistic future is still a largely unrecognized dream.

Some will point to the legacy of oil's wealth-generating side: paved roads, schools, hospitals and utilities. For too long, we floated, like complacent tourists, on a sea of oil money. Many might remember the $400 cheque sent to each Albertan (and many non-Albertans) from the Klein era, when apparently our leaders could think of nothing else to do with the avalanche of cash pouring into provincial coffers. Oil revenues elevated the sense of self-sufficiency and of arrogance, and created a co-lossal myth.

The myth was of independence, of unlimited resources, of future sustainability, of a world that stood panting on our doorstep, and of hubris. It denied the fact that exploration, development, production and transportation of petroleum was the progeny of government support; subsidy and bad policy; ineffective legislation; and weak social, economic and environmental rules. Even with a backdrop of miniscule and reduced royalties and rents (after the visionary Lougheed era), the public purse continued to build roads, infrastructure and other services to feed the black hole of petroleum interests.

Everyone was happy and content while the bubble continued to grow. No one wanted to acknowledge the volatility of the world market, the fact that oil creates a boom-and-bust economy. And so it burst several times, all within memory. In the wake of every bust, instead of a cold, calculating look at the industry and the public interest, we were all told to hold hands and support the petroleum industry in getting back on its feet. This, in spite of record profits and corporate resources that would have, should have, enabled the industry to weather these volatile ups and downs in the market. It was a great Canadian, and now an Albertan tradition – encouraging private wealth at public expense.

The delicious irony was that the mantra and mantle of free enterprise, of unbridled capitalism, was just a smokescreen for socialized corporate welfare.

The petroleum-era good times still nourish a nostalgia so sweet and sincere that there is a reluctance to speak any ill of it. Are we all complicit in this? To a degree, yes, we allowed the industry to write our future. It seems like it has been a long and lucrative ride, but in reality, it all happened in one human lifespan. It's important, if we are to salvage any credibility with subsequent generations, to clearly, objectively and honestly address the unfortunate aspects of the legacy of the short petroleum era.

These would include the huge, unreclaimed industrial footprint of petroleum development. Seismic lines, power lines and pipeline corridors criss-cross the landscape, affecting everything from threatened native trout species to caribou. Abandoned wellsites continue to vent more greenhouse gases into the atmosphere, contaminate soil and poison groundwater. Tar sand operations spew contaminants into the surrounding water and air and create a minefield of tailings and waste water reservoirs with uncertain reclamation. All of the industrial footprint is underfunded – or worse, unfunded – for reclamation, ultimately leaving the mess in the hands of Albertans.

The footprint of industry on the landscape is just what we can see. Largely unseen and underacknowledged is the invisible hand of the industry on our political systems, bureaucratic allegiances, media objectivity and academic institutions, as well as our collective psyches. When we take a deep breath of "clean" Alberta air to discern the influences, the pressures and the manipulations we are subject to, if it reeks of greed and gasoline, we should take note and, like William James, write the answer down.

THERE BE NO DRAGONS HERE
Mixing Myth with Reality

———

On several early 16th-century globes, when European exploration of the New World had just begun and details were sketchy, the cartographers wrote "Here be dragons" on uncharted regions. It's evident from the legends and the illustrations that there must have been quite a population of the beasts in the empty abyss beyond the reach of knowledge.

That dragons existed on the periphery of the known world and in the outer edges of our minds might indicate that they were in trouble earlier than anyone knew. For any creature, once it's out of sight, it becomes out of mind quickly, and the eventual slide to oblivion starts. It's dangerous for us to rationalize that a creature can always live somewhere else, when people living somewhere else think the same way.

I'm sad I never got to see a dragon; they were gone long before my time. Sure, I know they were dangerous, anti-social, reptilian creatures who had awe-inspiring pyrotechnic displays, but who of us can say they aren't just a little bit intrigued with them?

There is sadness in our wiping out of dragons. They gave real purpose to dragon slayers; to maidens who required saving; to those who housed, fed and supplied dragon slayers; and to the tellers of dragon stories. Dragons kept various locales free of wood choppers, poachers, trespass graziers, miners and those who felt that wandering everywhere with every type of conveyance was their God-given right. They defined the wild, gave measure to it and kept human pressures from overwhelming wild places. Dragons did this not only with their presence but also, some said, with their magic.

In the past, governments needed the magic of dragons, with several agencies keeping their budgets inflated for dragon control. Dragons were, to turn a phrase, the golden goose to inspire annual allocations for personnel, equipment, administration, travel and training. Then, of course, there were the conferences and workshops to share information on dragon-control methods. The last thing these people wanted to see was the end of dragons. Clearly, sustaining dragons, while managing the threat, kept people employed and productive, and the economy charged.

But there was a certain ambivalence towards dragons on the part of government. Keeping a focus on dragons also obscured what government wasn't doing, such as managing landscapes with a sense of balance and stewardship. Dragons and their implied threat kept the populace focused on them.

Governments have always used the strategy of "Look over there, not here" to deflect the attention of their citizens. This allows government to work unimpeded and unobserved on things that needn't trouble an unwashed electorate. Things like expanding this and that, doing it here and there and everywhere, pushing things through quickly, watering down the rules, keeping citizens out of the process, and engaging in spurious claims, promoting itself and kowtowing to corporate interests. Ironically, it was those very actions of short-sighted politicians and their business henchmen who revered the dollar as sovereign that led to the demise of dragons.

I suppose the direct and spinoff benefits of dragons, their value-added nature, could be assessed by economists to create a clearer picture of the role of dragons in the economy. It probably wouldn't have been surprising to find that dragons were worth more alive that dead, although that's now of cold comfort to dragons. Now that they're gone, we honour them largely as a distraction – on flags, insignia and coats of arms. What the world really needs is live, fire-breathing dragons, dragons that frighten, entertain and give rise to the substance of myths and stories.

The real myth is that we can do without them, that the pavement and suburbs and fragmentation of former dragon habitat ennobles and gives our lives meaning. We are not merely the random genetic mix of hormonally driven parents; we are also part and parcel of the place we live in and the beings who share that place. Paradoxically, those natural features and forces we find so threatening are the same forces that formed and moulded us. In ways often too complex to grasp, those forces of nature can preserve and renew us.

We are who we are because of dragons; our lives were enriched when they still roamed the land. The gap, the emptiness, now creates a void in our lives that cannot be filled simply with stories, substitutes and silly cartoon dragons.

To some of our ancestors, dragons were revered as representatives of the primal force of nature. They represented a domain where humans weren't king, a place of humility where we walked in the knowledge that we weren't dominant. Dragons were said to be wiser than humans. We won't ever be able to test that assumption, but based on the behaviour of our race, the answer seems self-evident. These creatures were often associated with water, even protective of water. Now, as we have used up many of the inherent possibilities of our world, especially its water resources, it's clear that we could use dragons again as protectors of watersheds.

Some thought dragons guarded precious treasure, or incorporated gems into their anatomy. Perhaps they enforced a certain restraint in our use of natural resources, a thoughtfulness not evidenced today. The lure of the treasures, of economic benefits, overcame our fears, and we slaughtered the dragons. We constantly kill the things that make us rich, not realizing that it is with their lives that we are enriched.

Dragons were gone long before we understood their role in the landscape, the linkage to other phantasmagoria, and their value to us. Dragon's blood was reputed to provide properties of wisdom and strength. We humans could stand more of the former. It is likely that dragons were part of natural disturbance mechanisms, using their fire-breathing nature to create habitat niches for other creatures. But we really don't know much about them. All we have are a few anecdotal references – usually from dragon slayers – about their bad behaviour. Methinks the dragon slayers were not an unbiased lot in their observations.

We didn't map their distribution; their biology and ecology are mysteries, and their population size and characteristics are unknown. Dragons probably needed space, big space, and we encroached on their living space and divided the land into smaller and smaller islands of habitat. Even the tiny fragments, the isolated specks of habitat, were too inviting for us, leaving them no space. Obviously, pressures on dragons and their habitats affected recruitment, and their numbers dropped beneath critical thresholds for population viability. Once populations plummet so precipitously, extinction is the next stop on the largely one-way train.

No record exists of efforts to reverse the trend towards extinction of dragons. Perhaps our ancestors' efforts paralleled ours, with status reports, policy frameworks and recovery planning for endangered species – fine words, hollow intents and masterly inactivity. If the present is a mirror to the past, the debate probably raged over the "real" number of dragons, a denial of their imperilled state, and concerns that dragons were impeding economic development. A thin veneer of concern was layered over a core of rampant resource exploitation, while dragons silently slipped into an oblivion beginning with the letter E.

Extinct – the word sounds like a hammer hitting an anvil. There is a cold finality to extinction. When the fire goes out, it can never be rekindled. Second chances have come and gone, the opportunities to deflect the trajectory used up, and the dice cannot be rolled again.

Neither our technology nor our prayers will assist us in creating another dragon. Perhaps when another heaven and another earth have risen, the chance will come around again. But the loss is in our time, and, effectively, that is for eternity. No dragon will ever rise again to confront our reality, remind us we were fellow travellers or challenge our ability to keep all the pieces. They only exist in myth and fantasy, and even there, only by a slim thread of memory. There be no dragons here anymore, and we are poorer for it.

Dragons came from moondark and shadow, mystical and ethereal sources. They are by far the most potent of all the mythological beasts, just as imperilled species today are often the most potent manifestation reminding us of our failure to maintain intact landscapes. If only imperilled species had the strength of magic and the sheer power to enchant and fascinate, we might be inclined to protect and recover populations, even in our busy world.

Of one thing we can be sure: dragons have gone missing. Other creatures, some as iconic as dragons and perhaps more charismatic, may shortly follow. Then there are the uncharismatic, non-iconic microfauna – plants, insects and amphibians – that disappear, unnoticed. Will we let all of these suffer the same fate as dragons, slipping through our fingers, beneath our consciousness, out of our memory and through the cracks in our careless world?

Dragons may be mythical, but extinction isn't. It is forever. And forever is a long, long time.

A LETTER TO THE FUTURE

How many of you have children, are contemplating having children in the future, associate with the children of others, or think children are our future? If you remain unmoved at this point, let me ask: Were you a child in the past, secure in the notion that adults were operating with your best interests at heart? I hope I've achieved some level of solidarity among you on the subject of responsibility for future generations.

I don't have children, but I have a grandnephew, Alex, and a grandniece, Monica. They are young and will shortly inherit Alberta, along with their peers. I spend a lot of time pondering their future. Based on my years of travel over the length and breadth of Alberta, my observations and those of my colleagues, the research findings of many, and trends now evident, I tend to worry about their future. I think it is paradoxical to continue on this growth trajectory and still profess that we want a bright future for our children. I have penned a letter to Alex and Monica as an act of contrition and to help them understand their future, if current trends continue. I hope I don't have to send it.

Dear Alex and Monica,

To you, my grandnephew and grandniece, I apologize for the world you have inherited from my generation. My generation lived beyond our means, but you got stuck with the bill for our excesses.

I can remember clean water that didn't require straining and filtering and chemical manipulation to make it potable. As I remember, there was also lots of it, but we conspired to drain, dredge and otherwise speed it on its way, out of our backyards and lives. We fought first with water; now you are faced with the prospect of fighting over what remains.

The sky was blue on just about any given day. It didn't take substantial faith to breathe in a lungful. In fact, it was a pleasure, but one we didn't appreciate. No, it seems that we Albertans chose to drive rather than breathe, and the air of our cities darkened with the result.

We revelled in large bank accounts, individually and provincially, with the administrative and geological luck of petroleum and coal underlying our feet. Did we save some for you? Not much. No, we were fearful that some alternative would eclipse its use, so we liquidated it as quickly as we could. We blindly mined your future, and you are stuck with the cost of that quick liquidation.

We invested in starter castles that spread like mushrooms around cities and towns and throughout the rural landscape. We commuted, often for hours, in vehicles slightly smaller than our houses, and just as fuel efficient. We complained about the high cost of living, but like drug addicts, we were really dealing with the cost of living high.

The soil that attracted your great-great-grandparents lies mostly buried now, under asphalt and concrete. What was left became too expensive to farm and was transformed into golf courses and equestrian facilities. We forgot that the basis of society is soil and the ability to grow things.

We lived in a province that should have been called Denial.

You have every right to hate us for our wastefulness, our lack of foresight, our greed and our thoughtlessness. Some tried to remedy this; their efforts were laughed at, their concerns were marginalized, their modest gains mocked. The name calling: eco-freak; environmentalist, the word often spat out as an epithet; and the ever-popular tree hugger. Maybe you can still find a tree to hug in western or northern Alberta. Concerned people used the courts, the institutions, politics, education and the marketplace to try and effect change. But they were up against powerful interests whose sole pursuit was profit.

Beware of the pursuit of profit that externalizes most of the costs to society and the environment. That quest is malevolent, and because of it the banquet of consequences is now set for you. I wish I could have done more. All I can do now is to remind you not to repeat our mistakes – something we failed miserably at despite the evidence in front of us. Ironically, civilization's long history provides ample examples of societal collapse because of degradation of natural resources. But we failed to heed those warning signs. I hope the generations that follow you applaud your wisdom, innovation and foresight. My generation was apparently bereft of most of these qualities. Erect no statues in our honour; we don't deserve them.

We were called the "baby boomers." In time, the strength of our generation would influence politics, music, consumerism and, unfortunately, the health of Alberta. History may show that we were an aberration, a cohort of people too arrogant and narcissistic for the good of this place.

We inherited a land from our parents and grandparents that was still rich in possibilities, opportunities and integrity. What we didn't inherit was their thriftiness, their understanding of community and cooperation, and their sense of limits. In my era, we called it stewardship, but we were too obsessed with wealth generation to understand the implications and the responsibility that the word entails.

We thought the frontier of Alberta's pioneers would satisfy all of our needs, and, unfortunately, all of our wants too. We didn't know – or wouldn't accept – that the frontier was gone. Because it existed only in our minds, we continued the headlong, heedless rush to get our "share." Regrettably, we did get our share, and yours too.

We ended up rich but with the type of wealth that comes without understanding, especially about the price of acquiring it. We cut and plowed and dug and drilled and built and paved like tomorrow would never come. We used up most of the inherent possibilities and fouled what was left with our footprint. We said we were doing this for you, so you would have the chance to revel in the wealth we had accumulated. That was our perverse moral justification for selfishness. As it turns out, it was the wrong measure of wealth.

I wish you could have seen trout swimming in water so clear they seemed to float. We clear-cut the forests, especially the old-growth portion, which held and stored most of the water that trout depended on. Sediment from the roads, trails, fields and cutblocks clouded the water and smothered the gravels. We built more and more roads for business and pleasure; in the end there was no refuge left where trout could escape hook, heat or mud.

The sight of a grizzly as it materialized at a bend in the trail terrified and excited us. It was a symbol of wild country, more elusive than a wisp of wind but a powerful metaphor for integrity, space and possibilities. We carved up the landscape with our roads and our activities until the remaining islands could not meet the needs of those majestic beasts.

Old-growth forest was anathema to our economic "wisdom," and as it disappeared, shrouded with the arboreal lichens that typified its ancientness, so too did the woodland caribou. They were derided by some as a species evolutionarily unfit because they couldn't change quickly enough to survive in the landscape as altered by us. On reflection, maybe it was us who were evolutionarily unfit.

I wish you could have heard, on a calm spring morning on the prairie, sage grouse on their strutting – or as some called them, "booming" – grounds. They were a symbol of prairie, as grizzlies were of mountains. But we couldn't bear to leave big tracks of "old-growth" prairie alone. Sitting there, on that calm spring morning, you probably would have also heard a chorus of frogs. They were an audible harbinger of spring, their presence a litmus test for atmospheric and aquatic health. The silence you hear now should fill you with dread about your health.

I wish you could have rolled in grassland dominated by rough fescue. It was Alberta's provincial grass, but I expect that now it is like the California grizzly, emblematic of our failure to appreciate what it meant. It had only taken rough fescue about 12,000 years to figure out how to survive in the face of fire, flood, drought and grazing. We came along thinking we knew better and replaced it with stuff that didn't know drought, didn't cure well and could only produce well with lots of rain. Been getting much rain lately? I think not, given the trend in climate. With fervent hubris, we thought we could restore fescue after we'd ripped up the landscape. We discovered that we knew lots about disassembling but precious little about putting things back together again.

Lastly, I wish you could experience space and quiet and solitude. Wallace Stegner, a prescient writer of a generation before me, wrote about our need for this:

> Something will have gone out of us as a people if we ever let the remaining wilderness be destroyed; if we permit the last virgin forests to be turned into comic books and plastic cigarette cases; if we drive the few remaining members of the wild species into zoos or to extinction; if we pollute the last clean air and dirty the last clean streams and push our paved roads through the last of the silence, so that never again will Americans be free in their country from the noise, the exhausts, the stinks of human and automotive waste. And so that never again can we have the chance to see ourselves single, separate, vertical and individual in the world, part of the environment of trees and rocks and

soil, brother to the animals, part of the natural world and competent to belong in it.

I'm sad you'll never find this antidote for noise and clutter and crowding.

Money can't turn back the hands of time to a world with fresh water, clean air, productive soil, rich biodiversity and space. That stuff can't be purchased. It can only be stewarded and passed on in good condition to the next generation. My generation's folly was to think that money could substitute for all these essentials. We were wrong. I'm sorry!

Your (not so) Great Uncle Lorne

What letter will you write? What will your legacy be, and how will you be judged?

Is my letter alarmist and hyperbolic? Is it too sardonic, unduly pessimistic or overly cynical? I don't think so. These things have happened, are happening now, or could happen in the foreseeable future. In fact, the future has already arrived. We don't acknowledge its arrival because it isn't evenly distributed just yet.

Perhaps a dose of reality about those things that are important will focus our attention on the task at hand. Robert Francis, a professor of aquatic and fisheries science, said, "It wasn't too long ago that my ancestors starved if they made a mistake by following their instincts to draw sustenance from the natural world. Now, if my instincts lead me astray, my grandchildren or, perhaps, their grandchildren will starve." That is the cost of a misstep now in our planning for Alberta's landscape and resources.

My instincts tell me we have exceeded some thresholds in Alberta, are advancing quickly on others, have no real remediation plan and are dealing with unrealistic expectations for returns from Alberta's landscape and resources. If we can agree on that, there is a light at the end of the tunnel. If we can't agree, we will simply add more tunnel until the light goes out. The public and shareholders may want it all, but that Pollyanna world doesn't exist. With time and explanation, most people will accept lower rates of return on their investments and lower salaries if these come with assurances of water to drink, air to breathe, food to eat and a place to live with ecological integrity.

Alternatively, we could wait and see how many of these essentials we are able to buy as they become scarcer and let the marketplace decide the outcome. The harsh reality is that change isn't necessary – survival isn't mandatory. No future is inevitable, but taking the future for granted, believing that it will mirror the past, is a gamble of monumental proportions and risk.

One can only hope that raising children inspires and motivates us to think of the future and the risk those children face through our inaction, greed or denial.

7

Places of the Heart and Soul

Earth and sky, woods and fields, lakes and rivers, the mountains and the sea are excellent schoolmasters, and teach some of us more than we can ever learn from books.

— John Lubbock

THE NORTHEAST OF 36
Thoughts on Land versus Property

———

By the conventions of how land is designated and located, ours is the northeast quarter of section 36. Eight hundred square metres, a quarter section, 160 acres, more or less, according to our tax assessment. But that calculation doesn't consider the extra acreage gained from ironing out the topographic wrinkles inherent in hills and valleys. Truth be told, we own more than 160 acres, but I'm happy with the flat-earth conventions of land surveys and tax assessments.

A raven's-eye view of the NE of 36 would show a steep ridge trending northwest to southeast on a diagonal through the quarter. A rocky spine lies partly exposed amid tussocks of native grass. Grassland prevails in the vegetation mosaic. Aspen forests flow off either side of the ridge, where the slope relents somewhat and snowmelt and seasonal springs provide enough moisture for trees to prosper. Thick willows find the wetter spots. A wetland formed by a beaver dam squats in one corner, collecting some of the runoff, and a small cabin takes up some waterfront property adjacent to the wetland.

When my wife and I bought the NE of 36 nearly 30 years ago, I thought we were acquiring property. Later, it became clear to me that we were in possession of land. The distinction between land and property has become clearer to me over the years.

Property is real estate and is tied up in economic values and uses, like the raising of cattle, wheat or potatoes. Land, by comparison, has a personality beyond deeds, mortgages and cash flows. This might include the topography, the variety of vegetation, the wildlife diversity and the play of seasons. This is not to imply that land should be locked away and unused but that use should conform to natural limitations.

A shallow depression from an old cabin, with some rusted woodstove parts and a dug well faced with stone, are what remain of the original homesteader. That and the enduring legacy of introduced grasses – Kentucky bluegrass, timothy and smooth brome. These occupy the deeper soils on mostly flat ground. The previous owner viewed the place as property and "mined" the grass before selling to us.

Before any of us settlers, the lineage goes back to people who didn't have a word for ownership, let alone for property. They did know land – its moods, seasons, needs and gifts. By comparison, us relative newcomers prioritize the extraction of its gifts, the ones we benefit from financially, but we ignore or give lip service to the provision of care that land requires.

The ridge rises a heart-pumping 40 metres above the flatter portions of the land. These slopes are too steep and the top too rocky to plow. Only a dab of level land exists. There isn't enough merchantable timber to attract even a "cut and run" logging outfit. The number of frost-free days is too low for a garden or fruit trees to prosper. The quarter does grow grass, but at 160 acres, you couldn't make a living off the pasture – or for that matter, anything else, legal or otherwise.

By prevailing economic standards, our land isn't fit to hold its head high. But does that mean it is poor land? Maybe the standards by which we measure land's worth are too narrow. Other virtues might need consideration.

To say the view from the ridge is expansive is classic understatement. To the west is an eye-stretching panorama. It extends as far south as Chief Mountain in Montana and northward through the foothills, the Continental Divide range, and the front ranges to the Livingstone Range and Porcupine Hills. To the east, the foothill ridges of grassland morph into flatter, cultivated land. Economic pragmatists would say you can't eat scenery, but you can be inspired by it. The landscape view that unfolds from our ridge still thrills us, and every new visitor stands transfixed, drinking it all in.

Native grasses, mostly rough fescue and Parry's oatgrass, cloak the ridge. In the spring, the dazzling blue-purple blossoms of pasque flower are a visual delight. They burst into existence from a winter-weathered, monotonous field of tan grass, becoming an eye-catching, colourful array. The thin soils of the ridge offer full elbow room for pasque flowers. On the slopes, saskatoon bushes burst forth with white flowers, followed, with luck and pollinators, by purple fruit a few months later. Sticky purple geranium with pink to lavender blossoms provide a summer array of colour, along with balsam root and its hillside wave of canary yellow flowers. Near the end of the growing season, the blazing stars, with their pink to purple blossoms, provide a final send-off to the growing season, a splash of colour before winter.

No one can argue these native plants aren't beautiful. But beauty is only part of the diversity these plants represent. Native plants have been thoroughly tested and have folded the storms, frosts, heat, deluges, droughts, fire and grazing (by both wildlife and insects) into their DNA. They have persisted since the melting of glaciers and are the bulwark against future climate change. Having them around is an insurance policy for the future, something that current, short-term economic thinking ignores.

The waxing and waning of the seasons are a reminder of Earth time. In our climate-controlled houses, businesses and vehicles, it is easy to forget that we are still governed by the seasons. Every season brings a new look to the NE of 36, and each is a tangible bookmark in the passage of time.

These bookmarks remind us of another sense of time, beyond meetings and appointments. Everything on the land marches to a timetable of its own evolution, from the flowering of chokecherry bushes, to the nesting of bluebirds, to the seed-set of three-flowered avens. Our schedules are somewhat arbitrary; theirs are programmed, like the daily timetables of winter birds, which appear to be a function of body size. Larger birds like ravens and magpies punch the morning time clock first, at about dawn, followed later by the woodpeckers. As the morning warms somewhat, chickadees and pine siskins, puffed up in insulating feathers against the cold of a winter night, finally rouse themselves to forage.

Spring can initially be drab, a study of browns and tans, with melting, dirty snow patches. Late blizzards dump snow, extending the waiting period and trying our patience – and perhaps that of native plants and wildlife – as we anticipate the release from winter. It seems like forever before the blush of green tints the aspens and the new grass emerges from the residue of last year's growth. Early summer is a blur of exuberant growth; of wildflower blooms; and biting insects. New deer fawns and elk calves emerge on wobbly legs, and nesting birds run an endless shuttle of filling insistent nestling stomachs. Summer turns to heat and thundershowers.

Fall brings on the most impressive colour palette. One aspen clone turns a rich golden yellow, while a neighbouring clone seems reluctant to change and sticks to green longer. Willows are a deeper shade of golden, arrayed against the red of rose bushes. Birdsong goes mostly silent, except for a few non-migratory residents like ravens and magpies.

All of a sudden, a northern front roars in and it is winter, complete with freezing temperatures and snow flurries. This is not an unexpected announcement of the finality of one season and the beginning of another. Periodic snow-eating chinooks reframe the picture, but only until the next blizzard. What leaves are left are blown off, and the white aspen trunks stand out against the perpetual greens of the spruce.

We watch, but we won't see the eventual outcome of the transition of the aspen forest to one that will, in time, be dominated by spruce. Spruce trees prosper in the shade of the aspens. A few windproof spruce stand as tall sentinels over the aspen trees, which tend to be clipped off by the fierce winds. Branches in the aspen canopy are twisted by the wind into grotesque shapes.

The aspen forest advances into the grassland during wet periods and contracts in dry ones. It is an age-old flux, a contest between forest and grassland. Willow forests occupy the moistest sites but are old and decadent, needing a rejuvenating fire to spark resurgence. New willow growth would be applauded by beaver and moose alike. But fire in settled areas is viewed with trepidation, and unless a wildfire erupts or we develop the courage for a prescribed burn, the willow will get progressively older and less productive.

In the aspen and willow forest, deer (whitetail and mule), moose and elk graze, give birth, and shelter from blizzards. Between wetland, grassland and forest habitats, at least 80 bird species make a living. Gray catbirds, several species of warblers, waxwings, kingbirds and western wood-pewees flit about the willows bordering the cabin. The beaver pond is a magnet for waterfowl and shorebirds, including sora rails, with their maniacal call. Grizzly bears cool themselves there on hot summer days. One hot afternoon, a sow brought her three cubs to the pond, where they played, wrestled and cavorted for nearly 20 minutes.

Pocket gophers leave earth mounds as evidence of their subterranean foraging. Cougars skulk on the edges of the forest, making the deer herd watchful. Coyotes hunt for mice and clean up the leavings from larger carcasses. From a diversity and biomass perspective, insects are the most abundant residents, although at times we could do without the depredations of mosquitoes and deer flies.

When I see a palette of wildflowers bejewelled with dew or a whitetail doe kicking up a rainbow of colours reflected from dislodged frost crystals, I have doubts about the economic conclusions that this is poor land. Economists might understand cash flows, but they make no room in their cost-benefit analyses for the intangibles that make some lands rich.

There are some who equate beauty with the acquisition of wealth. For others the beauty of art, nature and life itself are more potent sources of reflection, humility and inspiration. None of the wild residents, if asked, would rate the land as poor. Land like ours may not produce crops of wheat, potatoes or urban subdivisions, but it does inspire. We think we have rich land, and it motivates us to steward it, not for capital gain but for ecological benefits.

Relationships produce stories, and stories are a primary way in which humans relate and communicate. We have, over several decades, developed a relationship with the NE of 36, and that relationship is manifested in stories. Treating land solely as a commodity, only useful for what can be wrung out of it financially, doesn't lend itself to a relationship replete with stories of respect, caring and sharing.

Every time we turn to the land and walk its contours, we anticipate a feast for our senses. Some of our observations are from chairs on our cabin's porch – a natural, unplugged version of wildlife TV. The sights, the interactions, the seasonality of observations build a bonding relationship with the NE of 36. In the clear view of the stars, the glow of the moon and the enveloping silence are the elements of quiet reflection.

On the NE of 36, we begin to notice how loud quiet can be. Then there are the gale-force winds that sweep through the treetops like an artillery barrage. Often these winds send trees crashing down. A whisper of a breeze can rattle the aspen leaves. A grouse walking on dry, fallen leaves can sound like a troop movement of deer, causing high alert but no sightings for the hunter. When the ice on the pond starts to succumb to spring, it breaks into candles that tinkle like a light piano piece. On a calm, still night we can be startled to wakefulness by our own breath, although it might take some time to identify the source of the sound.

So much of what happens on the land is still concealed from us, because we either cannot or do not see it. The underground connections such as the mycorrhizal network between plants, an integral part of ecological function, can only be guessed at. Maybe only what we are prepared to see, or what concerns us, becomes visible to us. The wise bard, Shakespeare, touched on this: "In nature's infinite book of secrecy, a little I can read."

Although we are a long way from understanding the complexity, nuances and connections of the land, every year we add to our database and memories. We will never understand it all, but in the act of observation, we become more in tune with the land and its wild inhabitants. Maybe, in the fullness of time and observation, we will be better able to discern what is broken, what is beautiful and what is good.

Like other landlords, the NE of 36 has tenants. They are negligent about rent but clear on their tenure. Our land title infers that we are the owners of the NE of 36, but the wild year-round and seasonal inhabitants cheerfully ignore this bit of human legalese and hubris.

A robin routinely takes over the rafters of the woodshed for her nest. We are scolded incessantly by the house wren who nests in an old hiking boot nailed to a tree. A ruffed grouse seems to derive a perverse pleasure from roosting beneath the overhang of the outhouse. Its explosion of flight when disturbed makes a visit there a heart-pounding experience.

Beavers reoccupied and improved the wetland. In the process of rebuilding the dam and provisioning themselves, they cut down an acre or more of aspen forest. The opening up of the mature forest has encouraged aspen seedlings to thrive. These are untouched by beaver, since they produce a bitter compound that dissuades gnawing. Beavers came and then beavers left, probably in the stomach of a grizzly. The beaver lodge, a seemingly bombproof refuge of interlaced logs cemented together with a thick layer of soil, was ripped open one spring. Only a grizzly could mount such a demolition. These little dramas help us see that the NE of 36 isn't static; it ebbs and flows.

Grizzly bears bathe in the beaver pond, strip saskatoons off our bushes and leave their purple-hued spoor behind. Canada geese nest on an island, constantly complaining about the neighbours being too close. Chorus frogs, with their deafening mating calls, make it hard to sleep in on a spring morning. Sometimes at dusk, a moose will apparate out of the willows by the cabin, splash into the wetland and noisily slurp aquatic vegetation, oblivious to us.

Elk graze the fescue grassland in the winter and calve a few months later in the aspen forest. Once, a cow elk approached at dusk and barked at us in what seemed to be a general huff about interruptions to her grazing. In another memorable moment, a young cougar walked under my elevated tree stand, looking up at me with an innocent and somewhat insolent look.

None of the many wildlife tenants asked our permission for occupancy, sought our approval for use or showed in any way that they understood our ownership. Every interaction makes us less and less certain of our tenure and raises a question of propriety: Whose land is this? Ownership, as it turns out, isn't a human artifact of an individual or family; it is a matter of community, based on both the human and wildlife residents. We are resigned to the understanding that we are not property owners but are "owned" by the land.

HEARTS AND MINDS
Developing a Prairie Story

———

Two young fish meet an older fish swimming the opposite way. As they pass, the older fish remarks, "Morning boys, how's the water?" After a time, one of the younger fish turns to his companion and asks, "What's water?" The question might just as easily be asked, "What's prairie?" The point of the parable is that often the most obvious, important realities are the hardest to see and to talk about, like prairie.

That's why stories are important. They help us navigate the world, make sense of it, see our place in it and understand changes in terms of benefits and consequences. When it comes to prairie, we lack a single, cohesive, cogent story. What we have are myths – fanciful, flawed descriptions of frontiers, endless space and boundless opportunity.

Myths are things that never were but always are. They lead us, inexorably, to decisions that further erode the size, integrity and biodiversity of the prairies. We can do better – we need to do better – at telling the story of prairie.

Dawn Dickinson, a prairie defender, told an anecdote about her mother. She had come from the green lushness of England to join her husband – a customs agent at Coutts, on the Alberta-Montana border – in the early years of the 20th century. Writing home, she described her new home this way: "It has more rivers, and less water; it has more cows, and less milk; and you can see further and see less than any other place on earth." I would submit that our prevailing story of prairie hasn't changed much.

Prairie isn't just the space between the Canadian Shield and the Rockies. It is the glue that holds together most of the nation. In prairie is the essential space that defines us – helps us see ourselves, in Wallace Stegner's terms, as single, separate and individual in the world, while also being part of the natural world and competent to belong to it.

Both my sets of grandparents homesteaded in the aspen parkland of Alberta at the turn of the 20th century. To be charitable, they didn't know where they were going; when they got there, they didn't know the place they had chosen to settle. For many, settlement on the prairies was the ultimate in social and ecological crapshoots.

Once there, however, like so many others across the prairies, my grandparents started a transformative process of changing the landscape and themselves. What originally seemed to be a benefit, the woods and the water, were cleared and drained.

In living memory, the landscape produced a cornucopia of wild fruit, game and fish. In the photo archives of the Glenbow Museum is an image of six heavily armed men standing over the carcass of a somewhat deflated grizzly bear near Innisfail, Alberta. The image is from 1894, just six years before my grandparents settled in the same area. Yet nowhere in the family stories are there references to bears, wolves or elk, all part of the landscape immediately prior to their arrival.

Fish and wildlife populations initially sustained many families but succumbed to intensive harvest pressures and habitat loss. Non-native plants and animals were introduced, both purposefully and accidentally. The natural processes that drove and configured the landscape were modified. This has changed its character and integrity, as well as how we interact with prairie.

That is not the story currently told. The one that is told, for the most part a single narrative, is based on a myth. The myth involves real estate, opportunity, growth, prosperity and transformation. It speaks of the necessity of breaking a raw land, a land useless in its native state; of an economic imperative, originally to rationalize the building of a transcontinental railroad; and a political priority of keeping the land out of the hands of the Americans.

What has driven us is a gardening myth, one of lining things up in a row and making them grow. We didn't see the land as a marvellously drought-adapted place, a finely tuned web of life, and a place rich in biodiversity. We saw it as a storehouse to be raided and a place that needed squaring and replanting. A few early ranchers saw it otherwise, but their goals did not align with the prevailing mandates of political security and economic growth.

I can't discount that the transformation of the prairies, partly from my grandparents' efforts, has provided me and the rest of us a comfortable and relatively easy life. Comfort and ease breed complacency, though, and add to the perverse narrative of the prairies. This impedes progress on prairie conservation.

We thought the prairie was an eternal frontier; some still see it that way today, in ways both cyclic and perpetual. In reality, the frontier was largely gone by the time my grandparents arrived on it. A series of events with cumulative impacts has eroded the remainder and continues to do so.

So what is a new story? Here's what I think might be included. We've been given the gift of a common problem – the need to craft a better, more compelling, inclusive story. That new story might ramble between pragmatism and poetry, with elements of both. It must appeal to our hearts, in a visceral sense, and to our minds, in a cerebral way.

We must talk of many things. Fundamentally, the story must tell us where we fit in this place called prairie.

Dr. Stan Rowe, a prominent Canadian ecologist, pointed out that if we want to live on the prairies for another hundred years, we'd better start thinking about what this landscape is and what, ecologically, that means. It is hubris, he said, to "put our faith in technology and the power of prayer."

We must talk of climate – of climate change, of the range of natural variation, and most certainly of adaptation. Our story might be guided by the wise words of Einstein, written in 1946 in a telegram to the *New York Times*: "A new type of thinking is essential if mankind is to survive and move to higher levels."

In other words, barrelling forward with our eyes firmly fixed on the rear-view mirror is untenable. Acknowledging that there is a range of natural variation, understanding that droughts within recent history are really part of a wet cycle when viewed over millennia, is pivotal. That alone might convince us to consider other sustainable land-use trajectories.

History teaches lessons in limits. As Wallace Stegner observed about the limit imposed by aridity: "You may deny it for a while. Then you must try to engineer it out of existence or adapt to it." The long view says "adapt to it."

Stegner also pointed out, "Instead of adapting...we have tried to make the countryside and the climate over to fit our existing habits and desires. Instead of listening to the silence, we have shouted into the void." The prairie landscape imposes strong limits on human aspirations, but we routinely ignore and exceed these limits.

Just as prairie sage supports many creatures, the work of prairie sages – scientists, biologists, range managers, bureaucrats and ranchers – is foundational to prairie conservation. Our stories need to profile, absorb and remember the legacy of their work. Trailblazers include early ranchers who asked of their industry and of government, "What can the prairie sustain?"

We owe a debt of gratitude to these folks who grappled with limits and motivated the research that has set the policies and practices to conserve prairie. For prairie grasslands, forged in aridity, the wisdom of ranchers, long-term and profound, is simply, "The best side is up – don't plow grasslands under."

We cannot forget the rich biological history of the prairie. The journals of Peter Fidler, David Thompson and others provide a rare glimpse of the living beings who ranged across this landscape. Bison, elk, deer and antelope horizon to horizon. Beaver damming every creek. Flocks of wildfowl darkening the sky. Grizzlies and wolves.

In the decades following these chroniclers, less than a human lifespan, that miracle was largely erased. We created a new normal for much of the prairie. It's called shifting the benchmark.

We believe we're seeing the world just fine until it's called to our attention that we're not. Declines in quality and quantity persist until some tipping point is reached. Before that wall is reached, we all think we have at our disposal a full pie's worth of resources.

As our memory of the past dims, our perception of the present is that we have lost nothing, and our vision of the future is that we have kept it all. We end up satisfied with less and less, thinking we are achieving more and more. It's the resource that shifts, but not our perception of the resource. Perception does not mirror reality. It's a case of collective amnesia.

The past lives in memories. But memories must be kept warm: without rekindling, they can turn to ash. If they do turn to ash, we remember nothing, not the losses or the trajectory of future change. As Churchill is said to have observed, "The further you can see back, the more you can see forward."

Utah Phillips, folksinger, raconteur and anarchist, said, "Yes, the long memory is the most radical idea in this country. It is the loss of that long memory which deprives our people of that connective flow of thoughts and events that clarifies our vision, not of where we're going, but where we want to go." It is through story that we embrace the great breadth of memory.

We've traded the songs of meadowlarks and pipits for motor noise and traffic. We mined the new coal, the accumulated organic material formed under a cover of prairie grasses, in as little as a human lifespan. We did so without ever asking at all the appropriate times in the accumulating number of decisions: Is this the path we want to be on?

Not only has the landscape shifted under our feet, but something of value went missing along the path.

So our new story needs an embargo on the words *balance, trade-offs* and *compromise* if we are to avoid further prairie losses, fragmentation and loss of integrity. Most of the native prairie, including its wetlands and wealth of biodiversity, has been lost, compromised and impaired. We have an imbalance, created over a century of development, and that activity continues to nibble away at what's left.

What our narrative requires is a rebalance of development with conservation to reimagine the prairie's future. It will only happen with restoration – a recovery of lost space, integrity and diversity. This isn't advocating for a return of the bison, at least not completely. What should be reflected in the pathway forward is a sense of size, scale and variety.

Big trumps little in conservation. Big hangs onto nature better than small. We need to think big to save prairie.

Antelope, sage grouse, swift fox, blue grama grass, and fescue are all expressive of prairie – individual indicators of it and essential components of it – but not the entirety. Prairie is place, not just pieces.

It's not enough to preserve pieces of prairie; we need to reverse the continuing loss of this landscape and connect the remaining pieces in a logical form. Conservationist Ted Williams wisely said, "Conservation of what we have left is no longer enough; we need to start recovering what we've lost."

How can we convince people that the prairie is important, a sustaining sphere, a thing of intrinsic beauty and an end in itself? This is the place for tough talk about our future as prairie residents. It is also the opportunity to paint a picture of prairie that conveys a willingness to engage with it, on its own terms.

The glaciers receded 80 kilometres a century, 800 metres a year. We spread over the prairies and populated them in less than a century. Our transformation of them is arguably almost as dramatic as the leavings from glaciation. In *The Promised Land: Settling the West 1896–1914*, Pierre Berton wrote, "What we are dealing with here is a phenomenon rare, if not unique in history: the filling up of an empty realm, a thousand miles broad, with more than one million people in less than one generation."

We live in the aftermath of the Pleistocene, on the dwindling rivulets left over from the ice age, and are fed by the glacial grindings of old rock.

Life on the prairie is a delicate dance of life leading back, ultimately, inevitably, to that intermittent trickle of water, that cloudburst, the melt of spring snow, the reservoir of fossil water beneath the grass. History in the dry prairie is written on the thin skin of hydrology. Most of us who live here are a pluvial accident, wedded to rainfall. In *Wolf Willow*, Wallace Stegner quips that with another inch of rain or so, his sodbusting father would have succeeded at farming and the family would have remained Canadian.

Life on the prairies requires patience, cunning, understanding and nerve. Very few other places on Earth provide that sense of a razor's edge of existence. Strip away the delicate and often fleeting surplus of energy and materials that pay for civilization, and life becomes a matter of bare-bones survival again. On a frail mist of humidity rides all our dreams of prairie power and possessions.

Our power as prairie people isn't conferred from banks; doesn't emanate from politics; isn't based on cereal crops, potash or Bakken oil; and doesn't derive from nationality. Our narrative needs to reflect that our power grows out of the land, from an understanding that we live in semi-arid circumstances and around us are arrayed plants and animals admirably suited to survive and thrive. We will too if we emulate them.

Given the march of time, the elements that have helped forge plants and animals, the crucible in which they have been tested, and the variation to be encountered in the future, we kid ourselves that our technology, engineering and big brains are in some way comparable, even superior, to Nature's ways.

People who raise bison have realized that the way to herd them is to figure out where they're going and go with them. That lesson might be valuable to us to figure out how to successfully inhabit the prairie for the long term.

Maybe, just possibly, rolling the dice with Earth time is a better alternative. Learning to pace ourselves to Earth rhythms, reinvesting in natural processes, not taking so much, and doing without provides a more sustainable, survivable future.

W.H. Auden wrote, "A culture is no better than its woods." Maybe we are no better than our prairies, or at least what's left of them.

At one time, the wanton slaughter of wildlife was considered normal because there was so much. Today, the pervasive destruction of habitat continues, because we think it is limitless. Social opprobrium led to laws curtailing wildlife slaughter; when will recognition of habitat destruction lead to change?

Aldo Leopold answered that question when he said our tools outpace our ability to recognize how to use them gently, wisely and without destructive effects. He felt that only when we learn that the destructive use of land is unethical will we achieve conservation.

Random but cumulative acts and decisions by governments, industry and landowners precipitated an ecological crisis in the prairie of unprecedented dimensions. Sage grouse are part of it, and as a result of their diminished and imperilled status, we have begun to appreciate the consequences of our actions, many unintended. What is more disturbing, even perplexing, is that it all could have been avoided.

Rachel Carson, who started the modern environmental movement with her 1962 book *Silent Spring*, helps us understand why it wasn't avoided: "We still talk in terms of conquest – we still haven't become mature enough to think of ourselves as only a tiny part of a vast and incredible universe…. I think we're challenged, as mankind has never been challenged before, to prove our maturity and our mastery, not of nature, but of ourselves."

If one could imagine the prairies before the fence, the road and the plow, it would be so much sky sitting atop an endless horizon. Remoteness was abolished with roads, space was truncated with barbed wire, and the long view was interrupted with grain elevators, soaring above the skyline. Most pass through the prairie en route to somewhere else. It is only if you linger that you will begin to appreciate the prairie. It is not a place in between somewhere else.

How do we know a place unless we know the names of the things in a place and the stories they have to tell? We can't be sustained without a knowledge of the land. Embedded in the landscape are things beyond the surficial, the evident and the short-term economic value.

"We are formed by our surroundings, and our surroundings contain stories, that, if we learn them, form us too," writes Kent Meyers, a contemporary writer on the American west. "The landscape of the northern prairie, which seems so passive, changeless, and lacking in surprise, is in fact a place of power and mystery to those who know its story and who carry that story on."

To the uninitiated, the prairie has a colossal sameness. However, the sameness is not of monotony but of endlessly repeated yet constantly varied patterns and shapes. It is a prodigious repetition, without beginning and with no hint of an end. The prairie is an echoing reminder of time and space.

When you stand on the threshold of the huge natural museum that is prairie, you realize that you shouldn't enter without preparation. It isn't just about knowledge but more a state of humility. These are unmanaged landscapes cultivated by time.

We have done much to hold off the eternity, the infinity of distance and space on the prairie. We fenced it, broke the land, planted trees, created roads, incorporated cities and towns – anything to give the land some sort of human scale or distinction.

Yet, as Stan Rowe writes, "The wide-open landscape, the big sky, the singing grass, the meadow lark's song, the wind-waves that roll through the fields, the indigo water of prairie ponds at spring breakup were imprinted on me at an early age." So, in spite of our efforts to form the land, it inevitably forms us.

A stop, a walk, or a sit to ponder these realities can be unnerving, maybe liberating, and surely enriching. What we might find is a place where there is visual tension between the arch of the sky and the plane of the earth, where the wind tries to sweep you away, and gravity barely holds you down. The prairie has complexity and appeal.

In the words often misattributed to Edmund Burke, the 18th-century philosopher, "The only thing necessary for the triumph of evil is for good men to do nothing." I would paraphrase that to read, "The only thing necessary for prairie to go missing is for many of us to do nothing."

The mind has a way of making a detour around these uncomfortable truths unless it is forced to focus on them. To those who look at prairie as real estate temporarily encumbered by wetlands, native grassland, wildflowers and wildlife, I have no message of support. It is as it was, and always should be.

So who writes the rules for prairie conservation? We all do. Prairie conservation will be enhanced with a better story.

Who should undertake that vital task? Who holds the science, the material, the experience, the passion and the motivation? All of us are the new writers of the purple sage. If we work together with writers, poets, singers, photographers and artists, we can make prairie as popular as Prada, as endearing as penguins, as visually stunning as mountains and as engaging as dinosaurs.

Remember, the future isn't a place that we're going to. It's a place that we get to create.

ALBERTANS' LOVE OF THE EASTERN SLOPES
IS IN OUR DNA

In the early 1970s, on a university field trip to the coal strip mines of BC's Elk Valley, a small group of us listened in disbelief to a mining engineer's description of how the company was in the process of levelling one of the mountains. Somewhat in shock at his cavalier attitude, we asked if this was wise environmentally, ethically and, perhaps in the back of our minds, morally. His response was equally shocking. "Look around," he said. "We have so many mountains in BC, we won't miss one."

From the perspective of pure pragmatism, he had a point: BC has a lot of mountain landscapes – in his mind, a surplus of them. But Alberta doesn't. Our share of the Rocky Mountains – the Eastern Slopes and foothills – is meagre by comparison. They start as a sliver in the southwest corner of the province and widen considerably to the north, forming an elongated triangle. In contrast to the abundantly watered province of BC, we rely heavily on our Eastern Slopes, especially as the source of water for most Albertans.

For at least 70 years, Albertans have smugly prided ourselves on delivering oil to the nation and the continent. In the hype over oil, some might have forgotten that our Eastern Slopes have been the source of water, delivered to three provinces, for millennia.

Maybe our reverence for the Eastern Slopes started before Alberta was a province, with federal bureaucrats like William Pearce and J.B. Harkin. They ensured that most of the Eastern Slopes was set aside from settlement – for national parks, as game reserves, for watershed protection and as a timber source. A 1911 report by the Department of the Interior describes the Eastern Slopes as "a timbered area lying alongside of a prairie country hundreds of miles in extent...form[ing] the watershed for the river systems which water the great plains to the east, where water supply is practically the only limit to anticipated settlement and development."

These early policy decisions set the Eastern Slopes, as publicly managed and protected "commons," out of bounds for privatization. Without this, we could have ended up with a checkerboard of land ownership and an inability to manage that part of the province on a landscape basis. This sense of the "commons" began to percolate in the minds of Albertans, many of whom finally realized that these are special landscapes.

We Albertans often scoff at the initiatives of what we perceive as an eastern federal government, but watershed protection through "forest reserves" was one of this nation's great and (hopefully) enduring ideas. The Eastern Slopes Policy of the 1970s cemented in the minds and psyches of Albertans that these landscapes were important and had to be protected and stewarded, and that their maintenance was a matter of public trust.

Whether through history, experience or osmosis, Albertans have come to view the Eastern Slopes as sacrosanct, a landscape dedicated to the public good. However, growing awareness about the cumulative effects of land uses has led to simmering concern about unsustainable, industrial-scale clear-cut logging; significant environmental issues with existing coal mines; and worrisome levels of recreation, especially unregulated off-highway vehicle use and random camping.

The additional concerns about coal mines – with more mountaintops blasted off, stream valleys filled with overburden, water contamination, and loss of biodiversity and recreation opportunities – have galvanized Albertans. Why? Because they see that the future of these iconic landscapes is at stake. For many, this is a personal attack on something held dear.

Beyond the cerebral concerns of Albertans about the Eastern Slopes – water contamination, recreational losses, pushing wild species to the brink – there are visceral ones, not so easily articulated.

On a clear day the Eastern Slopes are within sight for many Albertans, and every day, they are within reach of all Albertans, in spirit if not in reality. Looking down on this landscape from above, we can see the mountains as a naked and serene backbone of twisted and tortured rock. Forests of conifer cling to the slopes and spread in an ever-widening band over the rounded foothills. In the southwestern corner, the transition is abrupt – from naked rock to forest to rolling fescue grasslands, in just a few kilometres.

The mountains, looming above a green foreground of foothills, have a superb clarity, even at great distance. They stand as sentinels in our busy world, a backdrop, maybe a backrest, for our emotions and dreams.

In the glare of a winter's day, there is satisfaction in seeing the snowpack build on them. Throughout the summer, I watch apprehensively as that white frosting disappears and stream flows diminish. Throughout the year, the clouds boil over the peaks of the Livingstone and Front ranges and up the Continental Divide, parsimoniously offering what moisture is left over after the BC mountains have milked them strenuously. We live in a rain shadow, which means dry, arid and parched for southern Alberta and drought-prone for the remainder of the province.

The winds pushing the clouds strike a chord, a momentary hum through the pine and spruce boughs, rising to a roar over mountain summits, racing down canyon slopes over exposed grasslands. The resinous fragrance of a hot pine forest is moderated by the sharp coolness of a streamside band of old-growth and immense spruce. This is a place that can remind us we are not far from our own origins.

When Albertans travel to or even think about the Eastern Slopes, we pass from the developed, the civilized, the tamed and the known to another place, one of unknowns, the unexplored, the intangible and maybe the mystical.

As a kid, I could look west from our farmhouse, over the Medicine River valley west of Red Deer, to the foothills and the "shining" mountains, so named by Anthony Henday some 200 years earlier. That country, within sight but beyond my grasp, was the real wild in my mind. It rivalled the mysteries of the Serengeti, the Amazon basin, the Himalayas and other geographies of a child's imagination.

Many Albertans can't travel to such exotic locations, but we can go to the province's backyard – the Eastern Slopes. Few things take on the prominence and are as important as a person's backyard and clean drinking water. Meddle and tinker with either (let alone both) and the consequences aren't trivial.

Albertans view the Eastern Slopes as our backyard. In that shared backyard is an opportunity to relax, explore and escape the developed world. Places in the Eastern Slopes can take on mythical properties as we search for personal space in shaded forest, amid mountain backdrops with the plunge of clear streams and rivers. This is where we find possibilities, peace and personal rewards.

We drink from the Eastern Slopes, we restore ourselves in them, they form a metaphorical border and backbone. They are our wild, our inspiration, and they are a place where we can see ourselves clearly as part of the environment, not separate from it. Why does this place called the Eastern Slopes evoke such emotions? Because there are memories of our fleeting presence there, of cherished activities, and, regrettably, there is also the trauma of some of the scars we have inflicted on it.

Many of us still seek passage beyond that gradient of the developed world and recreate exploratory journeys, mostly on weekends westward to our headwaters. Maybe we're like salmon, looking for our natal stream and a chance to be reborn. An older cohort of Albertans clinched their affinity with hunting and fishing trips. Newer generations camp, explore, hike, cross-country ski and birdwatch with an expanded scale of environmental sensibilities.

In a world increasingly mechanized, digitized, electrified and programmed, this is a place where we can escape to something more elemental, where our stone-age brains can better cope and find release. The simple act of building a fire restores an atavistic skill. The Eastern Slopes lavish us with many gifts, a few of them being peace, relaxation, purpose, strength, inspiration, challenge, reward and worship.

Sacred may be a strong word to apply to the Eastern Slopes, in the face of utilitarian views and users. But to Indigenous Peoples and others, *sacred* describes a place of ceremony, of medicinal plants and connection with cultural roots. Robin Wall Kimmerer, author of *Braiding Sweetgrass,* describes it this way:

Being naturalized to place means to live as if this is the land that feeds you, as if these are the streams from which you drink, that build your body and fill your spirit. To become naturalized is to know that your ancestors lie in this ground. Here you will give your gifts and meet your responsibilities. To become naturalized is to live as if your children's future matters, to take care of the land as if our lives and the lives of all our relatives depend on it. Because they do.

With the imminence of more coal mining, many Albertans have been jolted out of complacency about the Eastern Slopes. They've started to remember things they didn't know they had forgotten. Fundamental things, like where their water comes from – clean, clear and refreshing. It could be the memory of where they caught their first fish, a trout, which conjured up a place of quiet, of space, and reverence. Instead of a situation where we work over a place, the Eastern Slopes work on us.

Maybe some have taken a closer look at our coat of arms, with the bordering mountains and the green foothills that seem intact, but they harbour a suspicion that the picture hides an alternate reality. Others have consulted Google Earth and seen the devastation, the fitful black purgatory of coal mining next to us in BC, and wondered, Is this our future?

No government should overlook or misjudge the sentiments of Albertans and our deep-seated appreciation of the Eastern Slopes. Anything that throws open the Eastern Slopes to de-structive and unsustainable exploitation represents a serious violation of the public's trust and a failure to properly steward these landscapes for the public good. The cumulative economic aspirations, the growing recreational pressures and the accumulated scars show that we cannot take the Eastern Slopes for granted any longer.

Land held in common gives Albertans something to fight for collectively; there is strength and conviction in the crowd over individual, political and corporate desires. The Eastern Slopes are a gift from previous generations that creates an ongoing relationship and responsibility. There is only one way to thank those prescient individuals with foresight for this gift: let's not squander it on some short-sighted, short-term, get-rich-quick liquidation scheme.

The Eastern Slopes that Albertans want and need can't exist alongside deals shrouded in secrecy, bounded by an out-of-step economic ideology and an agenda rife with obfuscation and disingenuous spin. Much is at stake here, as we have seen in the reaction of many Albertans to the spectre of coal mines, industrial-scale clear-cut logging and rampant off-highway vehicle use.

There is a crying need to return to legitimate, evidence-based and nonpartisan land-use planning. Like a kettle boiling, the scream of cumulative land uses threatens the integrity and ideal of the Eastern Slopes. These landscapes cannot persist without limits set on the human footprint.

The stewardship objectives and desires of Albertans for the Eastern Slopes are still clear after nearly a century. It's part of our DNA. Albertans' message is loud, clear and unequivocal: we do not support the squandering of the integrity of the Eastern Slopes for a pocketful of economic mumbles.

Epilogue

God will not look you over for medals,
degrees or diplomas, but for scars.

— Elbert Hubbard

WHY I BECAME AN ENVIRONMENTALIST

It started innocently enough in a lineup at the bank. In front of me was a fellow member of a service club I was then part of. We chatted amicably about neutral subjects, and then he asked me about a land-use proposal that would have resulted in the breaking and cultivation of some native grassland. I expressed concerns, biologist that I am, about the loss of even more prairie. His demeanour changed, his eyes narrowed, and he hissed, "You must be one of those greenies." The conversation ended abruptly, but his statement lingered.

Greenies, fern feelers, tree huggers, eco-freaks, granola gangstas, birkenstinks, job killers, hippycrites, enviro-nazis, ecovangelists – the list of epithets to describe people concerned about the well-being of Earth and all her inhabitants is long and sometimes colourful. The time-honoured and often effective strategy of name calling and shouting at one's opponent destroys any semblance of coherence, communication and civility, as I discovered in that bank lineup. Labels are unhelpful, given the enormity of the environmental issues and tasks in front of us that require collective action.

The people denigrated with slurs and name calling include birdwatchers, anglers, naturalists, Raging Grannies, scientists, farmers, ranchers, parents and others who wish to breathe unpolluted air, drink clean water, maintain wildlife and support sustainable, ecologically benign economies. When questioned about their motives, all say they also wish to leave something for the grandkids other than an ever-increasing environmental debt and a toxic future.

You might categorize this group of malcontents as those who care, just not for stock dividends, corporate welfare or the ephemeral rewards of industry. As a group and individually, they write letters, donate, demonstrate, plant trees, recycle, reduce personal expectations and consumption, or do without. Even with a general increase in ecological awareness, they have to work to motivate, badger, coax, pester, urge and nag, to persuade people and influence institutions towards more responsible actions and outcomes.

The term *environmentalist* is often associated with such notables as David Suzuki and Greta Thunberg. However, most environmentalists work in obscurity and may not even identify as such. My neighbour is a committed recycler; a friend does volunteer weed pulls to stem the spread of invasive plants. Neither would call themselves environmentalists. The late Francis Gardner, a rancher and a friend, was clearly an environmentalist, judging by his actions, but he chose to identify himself as coming from the "radical middle."

Maybe many people haven't looked closely enough in the mirror, or into their own hearts, to see that they are environmentalists. Or should be. And that, by stepping up, they can make as big a difference as those usual suspects, or even bigger.

However they identify themselves, the common denominator is that environmentalists work selflessly on issues. Yet, as a group, they have been accused of acting in their own selfish interests. In an ironic twist, these people have championed decisions that all have benefited from, even the detractors.

To illustrate this, here is a little story that is a melding of many conversations I have overheard or been subjected to in boardrooms or coffee shops, beside some industrial project. A neo-con politician drives with a corporate executive to meet a lobbyist, who they hope will guide them in their task of thwarting some environmental legislation. As they drive, they rail about environmentalists putting up impossible impediments to "legitimate" economic progress.

Both of these people drink coffee made with safe, clean water, the result of environmental concerns raised and dealt with some decades ago. Their fruit pastries depend on pollinators, who are defended by environmentalists raising red flags over the use of neonicotinoids that are causing declines in bee populations.

A hawk on a power pole catches their eye. The banning of DDT in the mid-1970s allowed raptor populations to recover from egg-shell thinning caused by the chemical. Early environmental scientists like Rachel Carson raised alarms over the use of chemicals that bioaccumulate in the tissue of all living things, including humans.

The lowered emissions from their newer vehicle, which sips gasoline, contribute to slowing climate change and reducing the wild oscillations in weather that cause the corporate executive to worry about economic losses from forest fires and flooding. Fuel efficiency standards and reductions in greenhouse gas emissions have been the result of long, sustained pressure from the environmental community.

As they drive over a clear stream with banks covered with thick willows, they muse about an anticipated trout fishing trip, unaware that persistent lobbying from environmental groups has tightened up the rules for land-use activities, which better protect trout habitat. In addition, many environmentalist volunteers have donated time and energy to habitat restoration, including willow planting.

Both talk of a recent trip with their families to a provincial park, recalled as a pleasurable experience, with wildlife sightings, drop-dead gorgeous scenery, and quiet. Neither is aware of the lengthy process of having the area designated as a park, or of the environmental groups that championed the idea.

They are among many who are oblivious to the accomplishments of the environmental movement, and of those damned environmentalists. Acting as the adults in the room, we owe them for contributions to our health, safety, landscape integrity and transition to clean energy and sustainable forms of economic activity that work towards dealing with climate change. Just as we are asked, if we eat, to thank a farmer, maybe some recognition and thanks are due to environmentalists, instead of facile name calling.

So, with so many high-priced and highly placed people shilling for short-term economic strategies with large environmental consequences, it seems logical and necessary to have some balance, with a few clear-eyed individuals with contrary thoughts asking for some ecological equity.

With a gaze firmly on the economy, perhaps with loonies affixed over their pupils and the sounds of cash registers in their ears, some choose not to hear the truth in economist Herman Daly's statement that "the economy is a wholly owned subsidiary of the environment." We need to develop a perspective wherein the economy and the environment are seen as two sides of the same coin, with an ever-present feedback loop between the two.

The difficulty in merging the two is our economic system, capitalism, which is half a millennium old according to historians. As Carl Safina, an ocean scientist, notes, "Our daily dealings are still influenced by ideas that were firmly set out before anyone knew the world was round." Only very recently have mechanisms been developed to incorporate ecology into economics and adjust to the realization that economic thinking has pushed ecosystems into failure.

If we were to bring ecology and economics together, we might recognize that wealth is more than making money. An intact watershed that collects, stores and slowly releases water significantly reduces flood and drought risk, produces clean water, maintains trout populations and has aesthetic features sought after by recreationalists and tourists. All those features have values, many of which are economic. We can choose to liquidate that wealth through things like coal mining, but the long-term ecological costs and irretrievable economic ones will be greater than the short-term economic benefits.

The prevailing narrative of the name callers is that environmentalists are against everything involving economic activity.

In fact, most environmentalists are for many economic initiatives. They support an economy shifting from endless growth to thoughtful development, from the burning of petroleum and coal to renewable energy that would still entail tremendous investment opportunities and produce sustainable jobs. Other examples of economic activity supported by environmentalists are restoration of landscapes ravaged by inappropriate land uses, shortening supply lines and reducing energy costs by buying locally, as well as support for sustainable, regenerative agriculture. What environmentalists want us all to understand are the real and full costs of economic choices, not just the hype of inflated and sometimes illusory benefits.

One of the great fallacies in today's world, especially in the West, is that we can have our cake and eat it too, because the perception is that there is always more where that came from. We can have unbridled economic development and protect the environment; we can ramp up the extraction and use of fossil fuels and still reduce greenhouse gases; and we can have unrestrained off-highway vehicle use on public lands and still maintain biodiversity, water quality and quiet recreation. If it seems too good to be true, it is. Ask an environmentalist.

Wallace Stegner put it this way: "The environmental movement has had one abiding purpose: to assert the long-range public interest against short-term economic interests – in effect, to promote civilized responsibility, both public and private, over frontier carelessness and greed."

The real challenge, as Phil Burpee, a perceptive friend, suggested, is to remove the moniker "environmentalist" altogether. It is too handy a pejorative, despite the fact that concerns about environmental issues cut across lines of gender, education, race, profession, social status, geography and political leanings. We would be better to self-identify as "citizens" – with all the obligations that term entails.

Julian Barnes, a British novelist, touched on this when he said, "The greatest patriotism is to tell your country when it is behaving dishonourably, foolishly, viciously." When governments, corporations and individuals act selfishly, rapaciously and impetuously, we all should feel obligated to speak out. That's what I did in that bank lineup. It's unfortunate the conversation didn't go any further than me being labelled a "greenie."

The loss and diminishment of ecological integrity has been a constant throughout my career and compels me to think about the future. Are we justified in calling ahead and cancelling the reservations of the next generations just because we want to eat their lunch now? I hope the answer is self-evident. So brand me as an environmentalist if you like. I guess I am one of those "greenies." My lingering question is, When you strip reality down to the bones, aren't you really one too?

Acknowledgements

Writing seems like a lonely occupation until you think of those who supported, encouraged and nudged you along the path. Although many have, I'd like to especially acknowledge how I've benefited from what I've received from Kevin Van Tighem, Carl Hunt, Earl Stamm, Stephen Herrero, Duane Radford, Brad Stelfox, Jo Hildebrand and Don Ruzicka. I'd be remiss if I didn't also single out another group – politicians, bureaucrats and industry types – whose attitudes and actions inadvertently became the motivation and fodder for many pieces of writing. To paraphrase one of the quotes from W.C. Fields, "These people drove me to write and I've never thanked them for it."

I have admired many writers, but my hands-down favourite is Aldo Leopold. Reading his limited works, especially *A Sand County Almanac*, has given me an education in ecological thinking, a philosophical touchstone and the inspiration to convey messages through stories. Much of Leopold leaks into my thinking and writing because, simply, he said things so much more elegantly than I ever could.

Lastly, to my wife Cheryl Bradley, one of the clearest thinkers I've ever encountered, my writing has been made so much better because of your comments.

About the Author

Lorne Fitch has been a biologist for over 50 years, working mostly in Alberta but also in other parts of Canada and with some international experience. He has criss-crossed the province, learned the landscape, investigated fish and wildlife populations, and engaged with ranchers, farmers, industry and bureaucrats over conservation. His insights are the result of much scar tissue.

He is a professional biologist, a retired provincial fish and wildlife biologist, and a former adjunct professor with the University of Calgary. He is also the co-founder of the riparian stewardship initiative Cows & Fish.

For his work on conservation he has been part of three Alberta Emerald awards, an Alberta Order of the Bighorn Award and a Canadian Environmental Gold Award, with additional recognition from the Wildlife Society, the Society for Range Management, the Alberta Society of Professional Biologists, the Western Association of Fish and Wildlife Agencies, and the Alberta Wilderness Association.